CARL GUSTAV

Jung

h
10/06/04
14·86

Key Figures in Counselling and Psychotherapy

Series editor: Windy Dryden

The *Key Figures in Counselling and Psychotherapy* series of books provides a concise, accessible introduction to the lives, contributions and influence of the leading innovators whose theoretical and practical work has had a profound impact on counselling and psychotherapy. The series includes comprehensive overviews of:

Sigmund Freud
by Michael Jacobs

Eric Berne
by Ian Stewart

Carl Rogers
by Brian Thorne

Melanie Klein
by Julia Segal

Fritz Perls
by Petrūska Clarkson and Jennifer Mackewn

Aaron T. Beck
by Marjorie E. Weishaar

Albert Ellis
by Joseph Yankura and Windy Dryden

Joseph Wolpe
by Roger Poppen

George Kelly
by Fay Fransella

D. W. Winnicott
by Michael Jacobs

J. L. Moreno
by A. Paul Hare and June Rabson Hare

Milton H. Erickson
by Jeffrey K. Zeig and W. Michael Munion

Carl Gustav Jung
by Ann Casement

CARL GUSTAV

Jung

Ann Casement

SAGE Publications
London • Thousand Oaks • New Delhi

© Ann Casement 2001

First published 2001

 SAGE Publications Ltd
6 Bonhill Street
London EC2A 4PU

SAGE Publications Inc.
2455 Teller Road
Thousand Oaks, California 91320

SAGE Publications India Pvt Ltd
32, M-Block Market
Greater Kailash – I
New Delhi 110 048

British Library Cataloguing in Publication data

A catalogue record for this book is available from the British Library

ISBN 0 7619 6237 9
ISBN 0 7619 6238 7 (pbk)

Library of Congress Control Number: 2001131024

Typeset by Mayhew Typesetting, Rhayader, Powys
Printed in Great Britain by Biddles Ltd, Guildford, Surrey

Contents

Preface

The past is terribly real and present. (Jung, 1963: 108)

Jung's contribution to psychology and to the history of ideas has stood at the centre of my life since 1964 when I started my first Jungian analysis in London. This led many years later to my training as a Jungian analyst. I have often heard people referring to Jung's writings as 'mystical'and 'impenetrable', and am only too aware of the challenge of trying to make them accessible without over-simplifying the essential complexity of his approach. Related to this, it is vital not to do damage to these ideas by too hasty a summary and, while writing this, I have tried to keep before me what Jung wrote in Latin in one of my supervisors, Gerhard Adler's, copy of the first book of the English *Collected Works*, *Psychology and Alchemy*: 'All haste is of the devil'. This was an expression of his dissatisfaction with the finished product which had been years in the making.

It is also important to note here that although this account is written with respect for a remarkable man, it is not a hagiography but contains aspects of Jung's *shadow*. I have increasingly come to realize how important his own work in the area of shadow is for humankind's present and future. My own growing fascination with shadow aspects of psyche has resulted in my writing and lecturing about them. To quote Jung himself: 'It fares with us all as with Brother Medardus in Hoffmann's tale *The Devil's Elixir*: somewhere we have a sinister and frightful brother, our own flesh-and-blood counterpart, who holds and maliciously hoards everything that we would so willingly hide under the table' (Jung, 1966: 39). And elsewhere: 'Wholeness is not so much perfection as completeness . . . Recognition of the shadow is reason enough for humility, for genuine fear of the abysmal depths in man' (Jung, 1966: 239).

On the other hand, this book is not an exercise in desecrating Jung along the lines of the kind of tabloid sensationalism that has been written about him in recent times. Although it touches on the subject of the women in his life, it has to be said that there is no clear-cut evidence to support allegations that Jung had affairs with women patients and it is important to bear in mind that he was above all a moralist. Another highly controversial area surrounding Jung is the charge of Nazism combined with anti-Semitism and a selective coverage of the responsible literature on the subject is explored in the course of the book.

The Jungian community is a large, heterogeneous mix composed of countless numbers of people. The specialized practitioners make up a small proportion of this and, at the moment of writing, 2,300 analytical psychologists are gathered together under the umbrella of the International Association for Analytical Psychology (IAAP) which has its headquarters in Zurich, whilst many other practitioners are not members of the IAAP. These all use different titles to describe themselves, for example, 'analytical psychologist', 'Jungian analyst', 'Jungian psychoanalyst', 'Jungian psychotherapist', and 'therapist'. These practitioners mostly use the term 'patient' or 'analysand' for the individuals they work with therapeutically, so I will be using these terms where necessary throughout the book.

I have made extensive use of the 20 volumes of the English *Collected Works* of Jung published by Routledge. In some instances, I have instead used the Princeton University Press edition. These 20 volumes were edited by Sir Herbert Read, Michael Fordham and Gerhard Adler, and translated into English by R.F.C. Hull. They encapsulate the evolution of Jung's interest as it transferred itself from psychiatry through psychoanalysis and typology to the theory of archetypes held together by his abiding interest in the psychology of religious motifs.

I would like to thank Princeton University Press, Random House Group and Taylor & Francis – incorporating Routledge – for their kind permission in allowing me to use lengthy extracts from the *Freud/Jung Letters* edited by William McGuire.

A word of caution is in order here with regard to all the published writings of Jung, including the *Collected Works*. All of these differ from the unpublished original manuscripts according to the Jung scholar, Sonu Shamdasani, and, in some cases the difference is marked. Another point worth noting is that there are in existence more than 20,000 unpublished letters by Jung.

In this book, I am not attempting to cover Jung's vast opus or the myriad formative encounters he had with other disciplines. I have made my own selection in both these areas and hope the end result might stimulate the reader's interest in analytical psychology.

Although many of the terms that Jung used in his approach to the psyche are now in everyday usage, for example, *extravert* and *introvert*, these are used by him in a specific way. In order to elucidate what Jung was writing about, the book includes definitions of his main concepts.

Finally, a brief word on the writing style adopted in the book: in trying to avoid clumsy devices like 'his/her' or 'he/she', I have used 'their' or 'they' where necessary. Jargon terms are set in italics except for those that are in everyday usage like 'ego'.

Although I have been steeped in Jungian thinking and practice for many years, writing this account of Jung's life and work has inevitably become a kind of journey of my own. I am grateful to my friend and colleague, Windy Dryden, the editor of this series, for affording me the opportunity of re-discovering and re-affirming what drew me – albeit unwittingly, in the first instance – to Jung and to the world of analytical psychology. Jung's writing is the leitmotif that runs throughout this book but I am also indebted to the many other writers whose ideas have contributed to it. I would particularly like to thank John Beebe, Robert Hinshaw, Thomas Kirsch, Robert Segal and Sonu Shamdasani, who have been an invaluable resource whilst this book has been taking shape. The responsibility for the final product lies entirely with myself.

Ann Casement

1

The Life of Carl Gustav Jung (1875–1961)

God is the name by which I designate all things which cross my wilful path violently and recklessly, all things which upset my subjective views, plans and intentions and change the course of my life for better or worse. (Edinger, 1986: 32)

The Symbolic Life

Jung's whole approach to living centred around leading a symbolic life guided by the symbolic language revealed in dreams. In this way, the individual could reach a degree of self-understanding which would lead to a full and meaningful life. Jung's view was that any individual coming into therapy was ultimately in quest of a spiritual solution to their problems and that this resolution could only come through developing a capacity for symbolization. It is this that is at the centre of Jung's approach, which he called 'analytical psychology'.

Jung was aware of the decreasing influence of religion and ritual in the everyday life of most individuals and of the consequent impoverishment of daily life. 'We have no symbolic life and we are all badly in need of the symbolic life. Only the symbolic life can express . . . the daily need of the soul. . . Everything is banal . . . and that is the reason why people are neurotic' (Jung, 1977: 274).

Jung's definition of symbol is that it is 'the best possible description or formulation of a relatively unknown fact, which is nonetheless known to exist or is postulated as existing' (Jung, 1971: 474). Symbols are different at different historical epochs and, like everything in life, symbols have their day and then cease to be. Their function is to play a psychological mediatory and transitional role through which they can add to the personality of an individual and point attention to another position which may help to resolve an individual's conflict.

Poignantly, Jung writes about the transitory nature of symbolism in the following manner: 'We cannot turn the wheel backwards; we cannot go back to the symbolism that is gone' (Jung, 1977: 276). In this passage he is writing about the symbolism of the Mass in the Catholic Church and says that because Catholics are contained in this they find protection in the lap of the all-compassionate Mother. For those who have lost their religious roots, their souls become lonely and they are in a state of non-salvation and become neurotic. Jung was a life-long Protestant who tried to reintroduce dogmatic symbolism.

Symbol formation is an unconscious response to a consciously perceived problem and its origin is in the *archetypal* realm which lies beyond that of consciousness. The former is the innate, non-personal part of the psyche also called by Jung the *collective unconscious*. The archetypal language of the collective unconscious expresses itself through imagery, fantasies and symbols and has a separate existence from ego consciousness or the known part of the psyche. These two realms may be united by what Jung termed the *transcendent function* and he later spelt the divine aspect of the *Self* with a capital 'S' to distinguish it from the use of 'self' as denoting a person's identity.

In Jung's approach, the conscious and unconscious realms are seen as compensatory to each other and it is the transcendent function that enables the transition of contents from one realm to the other. It is this self-regulating function of the psyche which leads to psychic health in the individual but it is just this self-regulating that has, according to Jung, been eliminated in civilized humankind by critical attention and directed will. Unconscious material is needed for the transcendent function to become activated but Jung thought that dream material does not have sufficient energy for this purpose. Nor do unconscious slips because these are too fragmentary. Instead, fantasy is necessary and this must be allowed free play while the individual remains as conscious as possible. This latter prerequisite is an essential part of what is known in analytical psychology as *active imagination*. This will be elaborated further in Chapter 3.

While fantasy is vital to the above process, so too is the function of the ego, which Jung saw as being at the centre of consciousness. It must take the lead and must not be overwhelmed by unconscious contents. An important way forward in activating the transcendent function is the development of an inner dialogue. Through this transcending of opposites, consciousness is widened by confrontation with unconscious, symbolic contents. From a teleological or purposeful point of view, Jung argued that the transcendent function does not proceed without aim and purpose but can enable a person to move beyond pointless conflict and avoid one-sidedness and direct them onto the path of *individuating*. The *individuation* process is the end goal of an in-depth Jungian analysis and is the way of wholeness and distinctness from others.

This introduction to Jung's psychology has at its heart the idea of the healing power of the symbol. So central was this to his approach that many of his papers have the word 'symbol' in their title and two of the books of the *Collected Works* are called *Symbols of Transformation*, 1912, and *The Symbolic Life*, 1977.

Texts

Most of the material reproduced here on Jung's personal life is taken from various texts, including: Jung's *Memories, Dreams, Reflections*; Bennet's *C.G. Jung*; and Ellenberger's *The Discovery of the Unconscious*. The first of these has claims to being Jung's autobiography but this has been disputed by the Jung scholar, Sonu Shamdasani in his paper, 'Memories, Dreams, Omissions'. The reason he gives for his critique is that large tracts of what Jung dictated to his secretary, Aniela Jaffé, have been omitted. There are also telling 'omissions' with regard to the degree of unhappiness in the parental marriage and in relation to the seriousness of Jung's mother's depression. According to R.F.C. Hull, who translated Jung's *Collected Works* into English, Jung visited him in 1960 and told him that he did not want his work to be 'auntified' and that he personally would see that it did not happen. However, Jung died in 1961 before this could be ensured.

> From the beginning, much was made of Jung's omissions. On the one hand, Jung was much criticised for the absence of any mention of his lifelong extramarital affair with Toni Wolff, of figures such as Eugen Bleuler and Pierre Janet, and the vexed issue of his alleged collaboration with the Nazis. (Shamdasani, 1995: 120)

The latter, in particular, continues to be used as an indictment of the Jungian movement.

Thomas Kirsch (2000) states that the first three chapters on Jung's childhood in *Memories, Dreams, Reflections* are his own writing but the rest is Aniela Jaffé's, based upon the notes she took in conversation with Jung. Only half the manuscript is contained in the book because legal battles have kept the remaining material from being published.

Memories, Dreams, Reflections was published in 1963 as Jung's autobiography instead of as a biography. D.W. Winnicott wrote a long and famous review of it at the time in which he says that Jung's picture of himself in the book shows that he was suffering from childhood schizophrenia (Winnicott, 1964). This mental split was eventually healed, according to Winnicott, but resulted in a life-long quest for 'the self'. The theme of duality runs throughout Jung's writing and he recounts that at the age of four or five he became aware of another personality, an older man from the eighteenth century, as part of himself. He named his four-year-old self No.1 personality and the second No.2. Bennet suggests that this may have been the beginning of Jung's theory of the collective unconscious.

For reasons stated above, I have checked everything I have used from *Memories, Dreams, Reflections* as far as possible against what Jung said personally to E.A. Bennet, reproduced in the latter's 1961 book, *C.G. Jung*. Bennet was himself a Jungian analyst and close friend to Jung, who stayed with him in London in 1935 while he was delivering the Tavistock Lectures. Bennet, an establishment figure who was a general in the army and a consultant psychiatrist at the Maudesley Hospital, was a member of one of the first Jungian institutes to be founded in 1946 in London, the Society of Analytical Psychology (SAP). Bennet was a 'classical Jungian', that is one who has remained faithful to Jung's own teachings and found himself increasingly at odds with the psychoanalytic drift at the SAP. He eventually resigned in 1963.

Early Life

Carl Gustav Jung was born on 26 July 1875, at Kesswil by Lake Constance in Switzerland. Before his birth two boys had been born to his parents, both of whom died in infancy and so Jung remained an only child until a sister, Trudi, was born when he was nine years old. He grew up with country girls and boys, which, he claimed, gave him an early education in sex and led to him being surprised later in life at Freud's attaching so much importance to sexual matters.

Jung's father was a parson of the Basel Reformed Church and an Oriental and classical scholar, who taught him Latin from the age of six. His father showed an early promise of being a Hebrew scholar and married the daughter of his Hebrew teacher. Jung found his mother enigmatic because of her unpredictable moods and described her as alternately pleasant and uncanny. She spent a few months in a mental hospital in Basel when Jung was a child and he seems never to have forgiven her for her absence.

One persistent family legend was that Jung's grandfather, Carl Gustav Jung, was the natural son of Goethe and from the time in his youth that his mother introduced him to Goethe's *Faust*, the writer was a life-long inspiration for Jung.

Important dreams

At the age of four Jung had a dream which stayed with him for years. He first told it to his wife when he was 65 years of age and subsequently to E.A. Bennet – this is an illustration of how introverted Jung was. He recounted the dream to Bennet as follows:

> He dreamt he was alone in the field beside their home where he usually played, when to his surprise he noticed a square hole in the ground. Filled with curiosity, he looked into the hole and saw a flight of stone steps; down these he went slowly, with hesitation. At the bottom was a door covered with a green curtain, which he pulled aside. To his amazement, he saw a large, rectangular room with stone walls; a strip of red carpet stretched from the door to the opposite end, where there was a dais with steps, and upon it a big chair. It was not an ordinary chair, but a large golden throne with a red cushion, and on it rested what he took to be a tree trunk about twelve inches high. This had a red, fleshy top, a sort of head, not yet shaped as a head, with an opening like the eye of a demonic god. He had never before seen such a thing and had no idea what it could be, but he felt a strong wave of panic. Then he heard his mother calling to him. Her voice was quite clear, as though she were at the entrance to the steps in the field, yet he realized – in the dream – that she was in the house about 200 yards away. 'Just look at him,' she said. 'He is the Man-eater.' Here the dream ended. (Bennet, 1961: 10)

It was only many years after having the dream that Jung realized that it was about the phallic *archetype*: the principle of creativity in life. Another dream at the age of 12 was probably the most significant one of his whole life. He reported it to Bennet as follows:

> I was in the rather gloomy courtyard of the Gymnasium at Basel, a beautiful medieval building. From the courtyard I went through the big entrance where the coaches used to come in, and there before me was the Cathedral of Basel, the sun shining on the roof of coloured tiles, recently renovated, a most impressive sight. Above the Cathedral God was sitting on His throne. I thought: 'How beautiful it all is! What a wonderful world this is – how perfect, how complete, how full of harmony.' Then something happened, so unexpected and so shattering that I woke up. There the dream ended. I could not allow myself to *think* of what I had seen, for had I done so I would be compelled to accept it, and this I couldn't possibly do. So I made every effort to put the thought from my mind. (Bennet, 1961: 12)

He had a sleepless night or two trying to repress the terrible part of the dream as he was at the time a devout Christian following the religious teaching of his pastor father. When he could finally face the thoughts that came out of this dream he realized that God had poured scorn on the Church, his father's teachings and his own beliefs. The acceptance of this gave him the self-assurance that he was now a person in his own right.

The two lengthy accounts above about dreams illustrate the influence of these early intimate experiences on Jung. He was an *introvert*, that is, someone for whom the inner world has far more importance than that of the outer world of objects, and he claimed that what took place in his own mind was of greater significance than anything else in life. He exemplifies *introverted thinking*, which will be elaborated in the section on his typology further in the book.

The above dreams represent two key childhood experiences for Jung. There were other ritualized acts that were part of his secret life and helped him with his feelings of uncertainty about the world at large. He had a pencil case that was given to all school children at the time and in this was lodged a ruler. At the end of this he carved a manikin with a frock coat, top hat and black boots and hid this in the pencil case with a coloured stone in the attic of his house, which he would visit from time to time. In adulthood, he linked this ritual to the sacred stones of aboriginals and came to see it as emanating from the collective unconscious which is common to all human beings. It was these kinds of ritual that were highly symbolic for Jung and not the ritual of organized religion associated with his father. Wood carving was something he enjoyed doing in itself and, according to his grandson, he often whittled away and gave carved pieces of wood to his friends.

Student years

Jung was an indifferent pupil until his twelfth year when he fell and hit his head on a kerbstone. He heard an inner voice saying that he would not have to go to school any more and from that time had frequent fainting spells whenever he had to return to school. For a while, all he could think of was indulging his passion for solitude and nature. His parents grew increasingly worried about him but it was only when he heard his father wondering what would become of him if he could not earn his own living that he realized that he must get down to work. From that time he was an industrious student at the Gymnasium, where he spent his school years.

After school he was faced with the difficult choice of what to study at university and found himself pulled between science and the humanities. On the one hand, it seemed to Jung that if he chose science he would be studying something real but he was strongly drawn to philosophy and to Egyptology and was inclined to take up archaeology. Once again, Jung experienced this internal conflict as that between his No.1 and No.2 personalities and his worried father expressed it thus: 'The boy is interested in everything imaginable, but he does not know what he wants' (Jung, 1963b: 104). His father had been in poor health for some time and died shortly after, in 1896.

As a result of two dreams around this time, Jung finally decided on science and the thought suddenly came to him that he could take up medicine like his paternal grandfather. In any case, due to the family's impecunious state he had to restrict himself to studying at Basle University where he could do medicine. Even then his father had to apply to the University for a stipend for Jung.

The conflicting internal dialogue between No.1 and No.2 personalities continued but his awareness was increasing that No.2 personality was a total vision of life, of meaning and historical continuity. This connected him with Goethe's *Faust* and Jung became convinced that in this character Goethe had portrayed the answer to his time. From now on, Jung gratefully acknowledged Goethe as his spiritual godfather. He also felt this about Nietzsche's *Zarathustra* when he read *Thus Spake Zarathustra*. About this time he had the following dream:

> It was night in some unknown place, and I was making slow and painful headway against a mighty wind. Dense fog was flying along everywhere. I had my hands cupped around a tiny light which threatened to go out at any moment. Everything depended on my keeping this little light alive. Suddenly I had the feeling that something was coming up behind me. I looked back, and saw a gigantic black figure following me. But at the same moment I was conscious, in spite of my terror, that I must keep my little light going through night and wind, regardless of all dangers. (Jung, 1963b: 108)

For Jung, the illuminating power of the dream lay in the realization that it was his No.1 personality, with all its limitations, that offered the light of consciousness against the superior intelligence and timelessness of the No.2 inner personality. 'As far as we can discern, the sole purpose of human existence is to kindle a light in the darkness of mere being' (Jung, 1963b: 358). For now, it was his No.1 personality's task to take up the challenges posed by the external world – those of study, money-making, responsibilities, etc.

Interest in the Occult

In 1898 the time was approaching when Jung had to start thinking of which branch of medicine to specialize in. He was initially inclined to surgery but an incident occurred that changed this. One day during the summer holidays his mother was sitting in the dining-room next door to the room in which Jung was studying. Suddenly, the dining-table, which was a family heirloom about

70 years old, split from the rim to the centre with a deafening explosion. Two weeks later, a similar sound was heard from the sideboard and, on investigation, Jung found that the blade of the bread knife had split in several places.

There was no rational explanation for either occurrence. A short time later, Jung joined some of his relatives who were engaged in table-turning using his cousin, Hélène Preiswerk, as a medium. Jung's interest in the occult increased during the course of these séances and his doctoral thesis, published in 1902, was based on them. Its title was *On the Psychology and Pathology of So-called Occult Phenomena*. This was written some time after the séances had finished and was greatly influenced by the work of the French–Swiss psychiatrist, Théodore Flournoy. Around this time, Jung was also drawn to the work on the occult conducted by the English physicist, William Crookes, and by the American philosopher and psychologist, William James (brother of the novelist, Henry James).

However, it was Flournoy's *From India to the Planet Mars*, that was the model for Jung's doctoral thesis. The reason for this, Sonu Shamdasani points out, was as follows: 'In comparison to Janet, Flournoy posited the existence of non-pathological and creative components of the subconscious, and stressed that automatic activity, such as the productions of the trance states of mediums, need not be inferior to voluntary activity' (Shamdasani, 1998a: 118). Shamdasani's own three-volume work on Jung is in progress.

In order to disguise his cousin's identity, she is called 'S.W.' in the thesis. The séances would start with those present joining hands on the table at which point it would begin to move. S.W. gradually went off into an ecstatic sleep where she would recount on waking that she played a distinguished role in the spiritual world. Her name in that world was 'Ivenes' and she visited relatives or found herself in the Beyond in 'that space between the stars which people think is empty, but which really contains countless spirit worlds' (Jung, 1957: 33). Jung modelled much of his thesis on the way that Flournoy had written *From India to the Planet Mars*. In this way, he depicted 'Ivenes' as a psychogenic potential aspect of Hélène's, who was in advance of her conscious personality.

As 'Ivenes' she understood and spoke the language of the spirits, who still speak to one another out of habit even though they do not need to do so as they can see one another's thoughts. On her return from an ecstatic sleep, she would describe the characteristics of the spirits, for instance, that they do not study science and philosophy but are far advanced in technology. She also disclosed that she had been through several incarnations. There was a great deal of interest in double personality towards the end of the nineteenth century and

Jung was no exception. As we will see, he continued to be interested in it throughout his life.

Psychiatric Studies

In keeping with his interest in double personality, Jung had decided to specialize in psychiatry and in 1900 he took up his post at the Burghölzli Mental Hospital in Zurich under the celebrated psychiatrist, Eugen Bleuler. Here he undertook research into the nature of the psychoses and, in particular, *dementia praecox* (a term coined by Bleuler) or schizophrenia. Bleuler was a vital figure in starting Jung on his professional life by giving him his first post. If Jung had succeeded to the Chair in Psychiatry at the Burghölzli after Bleuler stood down he may well have stayed in psychiatry. He and Bleuler also collaborated on the project they shared in working with schizophrenia.

While at the Burghölzli he became interested in the word-association test that was discovered by the German experimental psychologist, Wilhelm Wundt. The latter's work was enormously formative of Jung's thinking, whose basic mindset was psychology. Wundt's word-association test was already in use at the Burghölzli in treating psychotic patients and Bleuler had drawn up a list of 156 stimulus words and using a stop-watch would time a patient's response to each. Bleuler became interested in comparing this experiment on psychotic patients with one on normal people and asked Jung to test several men and women in this way. Jung observed that the individuals were susceptible not only to external distractions but also to internal ones.

Theodor Ziehen, the German psychiatrist, had discovered the 'feeling-toned *complex*' in 1898 – a combination of images and ideas clustered around an emotional centre. Jung became increasingly interested in *complexes* and developed the work Bleuler was doing with word-association tests further in experimenting with them. Jung first became interested in complex theory through attending Pierre Janet's seminars at the Salpêtrière Hospital. Janet had followed in the steps of the great neurologist, Jean-Martin Charcot, with whom the former had planned to collaborate on experimental psychology before Charcot's sudden death in 1893.

Janet's concepts exerted a considerable influence on psychiatry and the rising school of psychoanalysis. Bleuler's work on schizophrenia was largely derived from Janet's on psychasthenia, where the basic disturbance is the lowering of psychological tension. Freud was influenced by concepts such as the 'subconscious', 'psychological analysis' and the 'fonction du réel' which led to the 'reality principle'. Freud was particularly influenced by Janet's work in bringing 'subconscious fixed ideas' back to consciousness through the patient's transference onto the doctor.

Alfred Adler's 'inferiority complex' derived from Janet's 'sentiment d'incomplétude' and the term 'complex', which came to have so much importance for Jung, grew out of 'subconscious fixed ideas'. Jung also became interested in other concepts from Janet like 'double consciousness', the 'lowering of the conscious level' and his work on introverted and extraverted personality. However, when Janet claimed priority over psychoanalysis for the discovery of concepts like 'fixed ideas' and 'catharsis', Jung and Ernest Jones attacked him at the London Congress in 1913.

Although Janet's work continues to be immensely influential on French psychiatry, his published work is hard to obtain elsewhere. As Ellenberger says at the conclusion of the chapter on him: 'Thus, Janet's work can be compared to a vast city buried beneath ashes, like Pompeii' (Ellenberger, 1970: 409).

Psychiatry

To return to Jung's work at the Burghölzli Hospital, the hospital itself had gained a considerable reputation in the world of psychiatry for the enlightened approach of its practitioners. Auguste Forel, Bleuler's French predecessor, had taken up hypnotism and written a great deal on the subject. By the time Jung arrived there in 1900, hypnotism was still being used as a treatment and he practised it a great deal and, for a while, was in charge of the hypnotism clinic. However, Jung tired of hypnotism as it appeared to him to be superficial and although he used it successfully in the elimination of symptoms, it in no way helped to shed light on the meaning of those symptoms. The latter was what really interested him.

Forel's other interests were also to play a part in Jung's development – for instance, he put together a combined social, psychological and anthropological study on sexuality. He was also a devotee of eugenics, the study of human improvement by genetic means, and was more of an extremist than the English eugenicist, Francis Galton. Forel's ideas in this area are the instigators of Jung's Larmarckian views as expressed in his writings on a racial psyche.

Jung's approach to the study of histology followed a similar path to the one he displayed with regard to hypnotism. He threw himself into it with enthusiasm at first and conducted microscopic examinations of brain tissue but this in turn proved unavailing in enlightening him about 'the intruders of the mind', as he called mental disturbances such as hallucinations and delusions.

In addition to this work, Jung spent a great deal of time talking to patients in the wards hoping that in this way he would discover something about the origins of their illness and what their symptoms meant to them. One woman patient had been an inmate for 40 years and was treated by the nurses as just another senile patient. She had a habit of moving her hands up and down and shovelling food into her mouth in this way, which the medical students diagnosed as catatonic schizophrenia.

On one occasion, Jung asked one of the nurses if she knew anything about the patient's personal history. The nurse replied that there was some connection with shoemaking and Jung was struck by the resemblance between the patient's hand movements and those of the cobblers he had seen at work. When the patient died, her brother came to the hospital and Jung asked him why his sister had been admitted to the hospital. He said that his sister had gone mad when she had been jilted by a shoemaker. This case led to Jung proposing that there was a psychogenic element in dementia praecox/schizophrenia.

Jung also continued with, and greatly elaborated, his work on the word-association test. This had originally been used as a kind of intelligence test but was of little use in this regard. Along with the time taken for a response to each word, Jung also often recorded the rate of heart-beat and respiration, as well as the psycho-galvanic reaction. The graph of such a test showed a correspondence between the verbal response and the respiration rate which, in turn, demonstrated that the mind and body worked in unison. In other words, the responses to the test depended on the emotional and not the intellectual state of the participant. Along with a colleague, Jung published a paper, 'Psycho-physical Investigations with the Galvanometer and Pneumograph in Normal and Insane Individuals', which showed that the influence of emotion can be demonstrated physiologically as well as psychologically.

In a paper Jung published on a female patient suffering from paranoid dementia he illustrates how he used the association test. She was an unmarried dressmaker who had heard voices slandering her for years before she was admitted as an inpatient. They told her that she was a doubtful character, that her child had been found in a toilet, and that she had stolen a pair of scissors in order to poke a child's eyes out. As a result, she often thought of drowning herself and was admitted to hospital in 1887.

The patient produced vivid delusions which were at first coherent, such as that she had a fortune of many millions and that her bed was full of needles. Gradually these became less coherent and more grandiose, for instance, she claimed to be Noah's Ark and the

Empress Alexandra. Over the course of two years, Jung took simple word tests from her but each stimulus word was followed by a prolonged silence sometimes lasting up to 14 seconds. The following are a few examples of her associations.

To the stimulus word 'pupil' she responded 'Socrates'; to 'love', 'great abuses'; to 'ring', 'bond', 'alliance', or 'betrothal'. The long time in responding shows that these are all complex constellations and the seeming lack of affect is related in dementia praecox to the fact that affect is deeply repressed. The extraordinarily long time in responding may be explained by the continual interference of the complexes, which assimilate everything that come within their orbit.

With this patient the three complexes that can be deduced from the association tests are: *the complex of personal grandeur; the complex of injury;* and *the erotic complex.* Jung thought that the latter may be the most important one but that it was displaced by the first two. This patient was also given to neologisms – making up new words – which is another symptom of dementia praecox. When Jung tried to get her to explain a neologism 'she immediately came out with a string of fresh neologisms resembling a word salad' (Jung, 1960a: 111).

Jung's approach to this patient, which demonstrates what a gifted psychiatrist he was, is encapsulated in the summary he makes at the end of the long case history he wrote on her. He points to the fact that the confused and senseless fantasies the patient has constructed in her psychosis have similarities with 'dream-thoughts' in their symbolic imagery. He puts it this way: 'The patient describes for us in her symptoms, the hopes and disappointments of her life, just as a poet might who is moved by an inner, creative impulse' (Jung, 1960a: 144). He goes on to say: 'In dreams he remoulds his complexes into symbolic forms, in a disconnected, aphoristic manner, and only seldom do the dream-formations assume a broader, more coherent structure, for this requires complexes of poetic – or hysterical – intensity.' These symptoms expressed symbolically become more understandable once the patient's life-history is taken into account. What Jung is at pains to show in his psychiatric work is how dream-formations develop out of complexes and how a patient's conscious psychic activity may be limited to a systematic creation of fantasies that 'compensate' for a wretched life. For Jung, the psyche works in a compensatory way to balance the conscious attitude.

There were several important results of the lengthy research Jung conducted with the association test. One was that this confirmed his theory about complexes which became one of his central theories to the extent that many years later he seriously thought of calling his approach 'Complex Psychology'. Another was that complexes were shown to be located in the personal unconscious and were not part of the realm of the collective unconscious. A further, related result, was that the experiments demonstrated the autonomous character of complexes which behave independently of conscious thoughts and wishes and which can affect objects and people in the person's vicinity like a poltergeist. The Jungian term *constellation* related to complexes refers to a psychologically charged moment when the contents of a complex are about to manifest in consciousness. This may be experienced as disturbing or exhilarating depending on the affect with which the complex is imbued.

Perhaps the most important result of the association tests was the part it played in bringing Jung and Freud into collaboration with each other. From Jung's point of view, the tests confirmed the latter's theory of repression, one of the cornerstones of psychoanalysis, which threw light on how complexes worked. For Freud, on the other hand, the association tests conducted by Jung provided a scientific underpinning to important parts of his work. As to the association tests themselves, Jung found the paraphernalia surrounding them cumbersome and increasingly boring and a hindrance to the doctor–patient relationship. He used them less and less and eventually abandoned them altogether.

Freud

'From the start of my psychiatric career the studies of Breuer and Freud, along with the work of Pierre Janet, provided me with a wealth of suggestion and stimuli' (Jung, 1963b: 169). In his obituary on Freud in 1939 Jung wrote that his work was 'epoch-making' and 'probably the boldest attempt that has ever been made to master the riddles of the unconscious psyche upon the apparently firm ground of empiricism. For us, then young psychiatrists, it was . . . a source of illumination, while for our older colleagues it was an object of mockery' (Jung, 1963b: 169).

Jung's first meeting with Freud took place on 27 February 1907, at Freud's home in Vienna, although the two had been corresponding for a year and Jung had been applying Freudian concepts in his work since 1904. This was illustrated in his linking the thought-formations produced by schizophrenics with dream-formations as he became more and more impressed with Freud's *The Interpretation of Dreams*. Their friendship and collaboration lasted for seven years, from 1907 to 1913, although Jung continued as the President of the International Psycho-Analytical Association until 1914.

Volume 4 of Jung's *Collected Works* is entitled *Freud and Psychoanalysis*, and incorporates his writings on Freud from 1906–16 with a couple of later additions. In the earlier papers on psychoanalysis, Jung ardently defends classical Freudian concepts such as the sexual aetiology of neurosis and the theory of dreams, including manifest and latent content, wish-fulfilment, condensation and the dream censor. However, even at the outset Jung expresses doubt with regard to the sexual theory in a letter to Freud in 1907, as follows:

> Do you regard sexuality as the mother of all feelings? Isn't sexuality for you merely one component of the personality (albeit the most important), and isn't the sexual complex therefore the most important and most frequent component in the clinical picture of hysteria? Are there not hysterical symptoms which, though co-determined by the sexual complex, are predominantly conditioned by a sublimation or by a non-sexual complex (profession, job, etc.)? (Maguire, 1974: 79)

Let us look at Jung analysing a dream according to Freudian precepts. We shall see later in this book how much Jung's approach to dream analysis changed after the break with Freud. The following is a dream told to Jung by a man of whose intimate life Jung was ignorant at the time:

> I found myself in a little room, seated at a table beside Pope Pius X, whose features were far more handsome than they are in reality, which surprised me. I saw on one side of our room a great apartment with a table sumptuously laid, and a crowd of ladies in evening-dress. Suddenly I felt a need to urinate, and I went out. On my return the need was repeated; I went out again, and this happened several times. Finally I woke up, wanting to urinate. (Jung, 1961: 31)

The dreamer was an intelligent and well-educated man who felt that the dream was meaningless and due only to a physiological urge. Jung asked him what his associations to the Pope were and he replied that 'the Pope lives royally' (Jung, 1961: 32). His associations to sitting next to the Pope were that he had been seated next to a Sheikh who was polygamous whose guest he had been in Arabia. 'The Sheikh is a sort of Pope' (Jung, 1961: 32). Jung says that the idea behind the dream seems clear: the man is a celibate like the Pope but would like to have many wives like the Sheikh.

Other associations to the dream were to the sumptuously laden table which reminded him that he would shortly have to go to the wedding of two friends of his. The urge to urinate linked to the fact that he wet his trousers at the wedding ceremony of a relative when he was 11 years old. The associations to the handsome features of the Pope were in particular to the nose, which was exceedingly well-formed. This was like the nose of a woman in whom the dreamer was currently interested. Also, the Pope's mouth was very shapely and this reminded the dreamer of another woman in whom he was interested. Jung summarizes this part of the dream as follows: he says that the 'Pope' is a good example of condensation in synthesizing the dreamer because of his celibate life, but also the polygamous Sheikh. He is also two women in whom the dreamer is interested and the associations to weddings are linked to these.

The later papers increasingly show Jung's growing criticism of psychoanalysis and, in particular, of the sexual theory. In a paper on the Oedipus complex and the problem of incest, Jung puts forward his own theory as follows: 'Here religion is a great help because, by the bridge of the symbol, it leads his libido away from the infantile objects (parents) towards the symbolic representatives of the past' (Jung, 1961: 156).

The paper ends on a note of complete rejection of Freud's Oedipus complex:

> He therefore takes the tendency towards incest to be an absolutely concrete sexual wish, for he calls this complex the root-complex, or nucleus, of the neuroses and is inclined, viewing this as the original one, to reduce practically the whole psychology of the neuroses, as well as many other phenomena in the realm of the mind, to this one complex. (Jung, 1961: 156)

Sexual theory

In *Memories, Dreams, Reflections* Jung says that he had doubts from the beginning about Freud's theory that sexual repression and trauma were the cause of all neuroses. However, because he felt that Freud had opened up a new path of investigation, Jung tried to suppress his own misgivings. He says that on occasion when he tried to air them Freud would attribute these to Jung's lack of experience.

On one occasion in 1910 Jung recalls Freud saying to him: 'My dear Jung, promise me never to abandon the sexual theory. That is the most essential thing of all. You see, we must make a dogma of it, an unshakable bulwark.'

Jung asked what it was a bulwark against and Freud famously replied: 'Against the black tide of mud of occultism' (Jung, 1963b: 173). This confirmed Jung's intuition that for Freud sexuality was a sort of '*numinosum*' – that is a tremendous and compelling force akin to religious experience. 'Freud, who had always made much of his irreligiosity, had now constructed a dogma; or rather, in the place of a jealous God whom he had lost, he had substituted another compelling image, that of sexuality' (Jung, 1963b: 174).

In the early 1900s when Jung was first coming in contact with Freud's ideas, the latter was still *persona non grata* in academic and scientific circles. Jung himself had mixed feelings about the fact that his association experiments were in agreement with Freud's theories and was tempted to publish his conclusions without mentioning Freud's name. But then he heard the voice of No.2 personality saying: 'If you do a thing like that, as if you had no knowledge of Freud, it would be a piece of trickery. You cannot build your life upon a lie' (Jung, 1963b: 171).

Heir Apparent

From this time on, Jung became an open supporter of Freud and in 1906 published a paper, 'Freud's Theory of Hysteria: A Reply to Aschaffenburg', supporting him. He was warned by two German professors that he was endangering his academic career but nevertheless went on defending Freud. In 1907, the latter invited Jung and his wife to visit him in Vienna. As this was one of the great meetings of minds of the last century, I will give two brief accounts of it – one from the Jungian perspective, the other from the Freudian.

> Jung in his turn was eager to know Freud, and he records that he was the most remarkable person he had then met. Their first talk, in Freud's house, lasted for thirteen hours! . . . According to Jung, the talk was protracted because he continued to question Freud, hoping to get beyond these limitations, and in particular Freud's insistence on the importance of the infantile sexual trauma as a settled, unalterable basis of his work. (Bennet, 1961: 33)

In July 1907 at the International Congress of Neurology in Amsterdam:

> Jung gave me a lively account of his first interview (with Freud). He had very much to tell Freud and to ask him, and with intense animation he poured forth in a spate for three whole hours. Then the patient, absorbed listener interrupted him with the suggestion that they conduct their discussion more systematically. To Jung's great astonishment Freud proceeded to group the contents of the harangue under several precise headings that enabled them to spend the further hours in a more profitable give and take. (Jones, 1955: 36)

Their mutual admiration after this first meeting was unbounded and Jung declared that Freud was handsome and asked his wife to send him – Jung – a photograph of Freud. To continue with Jones's account, Jung regarded this meeting as the high point of his life (confirmed by Bennet) and said that: 'whoever had acquired a knowledge of psychoanalysis had eaten of the tree of Paradise and attained vision' (Jones, 1955: 37).

Freud, for his part, was equally inspired and grateful to have the support of an aryan as he wanted psychoanalysis to be opened up to the non-Jewish world. He claimed that Jung was one of the only two original minds among his followers.

> He soon decided that Jung was to be his successor and at times called him his 'son and heir' . . . Jung was to be the Joshua destined to explore the promised land of psychiatry which Freud, like Moses, was only permitted to view from afar. Incidentally, this remark is of interest as indicating Freud's self-identification with Moses, one which in later years became very evident. (Jones, 1955: 37)

There are strong undertones of an idealized father/son transference and countertransference in which both men appear to have been swept up at the moment of their first meeting.

> Freud and Jung were to come together on nine or ten further occasions, including four Congresses and the journey to America together, but the freshness of the first meeting could never be experienced again. The last time they saw each other was at the Munich Congress in September, 1913. (Jones, 1955: 38)

Two years later they met again in Vienna and were talking of the psychoanalytic movement in Freud's study. According to the account Jung gave Bennet of this encounter he was for the first time finding Freud unyielding and their association almost impossible. During this discussion, they were both startled to hear a formidable crash as if the bookcase in the room was about to fall down. Jung said, 'It will happen again,' – at which point it did. When they both examined the bookcase they could find nothing. This event represented for Jung a parapsychological phenomenon. He says that he tried to discuss it with Freud as a synchronistic event, that is one not explainable by cause and effect, which might augur a split between the two of them. However, Freud refused to take it seriously and dismissed the whole matter.

Jones's account of this affair is again somewhat different:

> On one of his first visits to Vienna on March 25, 1909, he (Jung) regaled Freud one evening with astonishing stories of his experiences, and also displayed his powers as a poltergeist by making various articles in the room rattle on the furniture. (Jones, 1957: 411)

However, Jung, Freud and Jones are in agreement in being unimpressed by the followers that Freud surrounded himself with in Vienna.

Jung had told me in Zurich what a pity it was that Freud had no followers of any weight in Vienna, and that he was surrounded there by a 'degenerate and Bohemian crowd' who did him little credit. (Jones, 1959: 169–70)

The reader may perhaps gather that I was not highly impressed with the assembly. It seemed an unworthy accompaniment to Freud's genius, but in the Vienna of those days, so full of prejudice against him, it was hard to secure a pupil with a reputation to lose, so he had to take what he could get. (Jones, 1959: 169–70)

I [Freud] no longer get any pleasure from the Viennese. I have a heavy cross to bear with the older generation, Stekel, Adler, Sadger. (Jones, 1955: 78)

Jones did, however, impute the antagonism between Jung and the Vienna Group to the former's anti-Semitic streak. John Kerr in his book *A Most Dangerous Method*, named after a saying by William James with regard to psychoanalysis, says that this charge is unfair:

At the time of his first visit, Jung was still in the grip of what can best be described as his Jewish romance. He was positively attracted by the Jewishness of psychoanalysis . . . Having early abandoned Swiss Calvinism, the faith he was raised in, Jung was without a church of his own; for him Judaism, like occultism, was an intriguing church next door. (Kerr, 1994: 133)

Freud came to rely on Jung increasingly and made him the editor of the *The Yearbook for Psychoanalytic and Psychopathological Researches*, which had its first edition in 1909. At the second Psychoanalytic Congress held at Nuremberg in 1910, the International Psychoanalytic Association (IPA) was founded and Freud's initial idea was to appoint Jung as the president in perpetuity, with complete power to appoint and remove analysts. Wittels's biography of Freud gives a glimpse of how the Viennese analysts reacted to this, for instance, Alfred Adler and Wilhelm Stekel were utterly dismayed as it meant that from then on analysts would have to submit their scientific writings to Jung for approval before publication (Wittels, 1934). Further, the future development of psychoanalysis would lie in Jung's and not Freud's hands.

The Viennese analysts held a private meeting in the Grand Hotel at Nuremberg to discuss the new situation and Freud made an unexpected appearance. He burst into an excited speech, as follows:

Most of you are Jews, and therefore you are incompetent to win friends for the new teaching. Jews must be content with the modest rôle of preparing the ground. It is absolutely essential that I should form ties in the world of general science. I am getting on in years, and am weary of being perpetually attacked. We are all in danger. [Seizing his coat by the lapels, he said:] They won't even leave me a coat on my back. The Swiss will save us – will save me, and all of you as well. (Wittels, 1934: 12)

The furore all this caused, particularly amongst the Viennese analysts, resulted in a modification of the original proposals. Jung was made president for two years and the official seat of the IPA was to be in Zurich for the duration of his presidency. Alfred Adler was made president of the Vienna Society. The organizational birth of the psychoanalytical movement was fraught with difficulties on all sides and even Bleuler refused to join. By August 1910, Freud had expressed doubts but was reassured by Jung in such a heartening way that the founding of the IPA had one positive outcome: that of reconciling them to each other after the tensions engendered by the American trip described below.

America

According to Jung, the year 1909 proved to be a decisive one for his relationship with Freud. The two had been invited to lecture at Clark University in Worcester, Massachusetts and they decided to travel together with Sandor Ferenczi accompanying them. They met up in Bremen and, according to Jung's account, this was where the famous fainting fit of Freud's occurred. It was provoked by a discussion on the prehistoric 'peat-bog corpses' which are to be found in northern Germany. Jung seems to have discussed these on several occasions, including once at the dinner table during which Freud became agitated and suddenly fainted. Later, he interpreted Jung's fascination with corpses as a death-wish against himself.

Freud fainted another time in Jung's presence during the Psychoanalytic Congress in Munich in 1912. This time the discussion centred on the monotheistic Ancient Egyptian Pharaoh, Akhenaten. Jung disputed strongly against those who interpreted Akhenaten's monotheism as a personal resistance to his father because he had obliterated his father's names from statues. At this point, Freud slid off his chair in a faint and Jung picked him up and carried him to a sofa in the next room. Jung attributes both instances of fainting to Freud's fantasy of father-murder.

Jung says that though Freud made frequent allusions to him as his successor, he himself was not greatly enamoured of the idea as he had no real desire to be the leader of the movement. He declares that it was not in his nature to be that and that he felt it would mean sacrificing his intellectual independence. We will revisit this point later and, in the meantime, let us return to the visit to America.

Jung and Freud spent seven weeks in the USA where they were together every day. As a result, they took to analysing each other's dreams but something occurred one day which 'proved to be a severe blow to the whole relationship' (Jung, 1963b: 181). Freud had a dream which Jung interpreted and then asked for more information about the former's private life in order to interpret it in more depth. Jung reports that Freud's response was to look at him with suspicion and say: 'But I cannot risk my authority' (Jung, 1963b: 182). At this point Jung says that in his eyes Freud lost his authority for placing himself above truth.

It was during the American trip that Jung had a dream that was to give him the first intimation of his theory of the collective unconscious. It went as follows:

> I was in a house I did not know, which had two storeys. It was 'my house'. I found myself in the upper storey, where there was a kind of salon furnished with fine old pieces in rococo style. On the walls hung a number of precious old paintings. I wondered that this should be my house, and thought, 'Not bad'. But then it occurred to me that I did not know what the lower floor looked like. Descending the stairs, I reached the ground floor. There everything was much older, and I realized that this part of the house must date from about the fifteenth or sixteenth century. The furnishings were medieval; the floors were of red brick. Everywhere it was rather dark. I went from one room to another, thinking, 'Now I really must explore the whole house'. I came upon a heavy door, and opened it. Beyond it, I discovered a stone stairway that led down into the cellar. Descending again, I found myself in a beautifully vaulted room which looked exceedingly ancient. Examining the walls, I discovered layers of brick among the ordinary stone blocks, and chips of brick in the mortar. As soon as I saw this I knew that the walls dated from Roman times. My interest by now was intense. I looked more closely at the floor. It was on stone slabs, and in one of these I discovered a ring. When I pulled it, the stone slab lifted, and again I saw a stairway of narrow stone steps leading down into the depths. These, too, I descended, and entered a low cave cut into the rock. Thick dust lay on the floor, and in the dust were scattered bones and broken pottery, like remains of a primitive culture. I discovered two human skulls, obviously very old and half disintegrated. (Jung, 1963b: 183)

Jung told this dream to Freud, who returned repeatedly to the theme of the skulls, asking for Jung's associations with them. Jung says that he knew that Freud was thinking again of death-wishes against himself so, in order to deflect this, Jung lied and said that he associated them with his wife and sister-in-law.

Jung's own interpretation of the dream was that it represented an image of the psyche: the first floor standing for his conscious state; the ground floor for the first level of unconsciousness and so on. He saw the cave as representing the most primitive layer of psyche bordering on the animal soul. For Jung, the dream contained the history of successive layers of consciousness.

It was these kinds of incidents that started to show up the growing rift between Freud and Jung and the strain engendered by the unknown that the USA represented added to their tensions. A.A. Brill met them in New York and took them on expeditions to Chinatown and Central Park. From New York, Freud, Jung, Ferenczi and Brill went to Worcester for the Congress. Their host was Stanley Hall, who had been William James's star pupil at Harvard in the study of physiological psychology. Ernest Jones was also there bringing with him James Jackson Putnam, holder of the first American Chair in neurology at Harvard. Freud and Jung had a huge success at the Congress and their American audiences were enormously interested to hear more about psychoanalysis and the experiments with complexes. Freud's conflict theory – 'libido' versus 'repression' – was seen as shedding much-needed light in explaining Janet's constitutional theory of hereditary weakness combined with moral degeneration as progenitors of hysterical symptoms.

Both Freud and Jung were gratified at the adulation with which such sophisticated audiences greeted their lectures and they were awarded honorary degrees at the end of the Congress. William James remained sceptical saying:

> I confess that he (Freud) made on me personally the impression of a man obsessed with fixed ideas. I can make nothing in my own case with his dream theories, and obviously 'symbolism' is a most dangerous method. (Kerr, 1994: 245)

Letters

The best witness to the nature of the collaboration between Freud and Jung is the lengthy correspondence between them from the years 1906 to 1913. The first actual letter was written by Freud on 11 April 1906, warmly acknowledging a volume sent to him by Jung. Their letters to each other remained unpublished until after the death of both men and as late as 1959, two years before Jung's death, he was interviewed by John Freeman for the BBC as follows:

> *Freeman*: When are the letters which you exchanged with Freud going to be published?
> *Jung*: Well, not during my lifetime.
> *Freeman*: You would have no objection to their being published after your lifetime?
> *Jung*: Oh, no, none at all.
> *Freeman*: Because they are probably of great historical importance.

Jung: I don't think so.
Freeman: Then why have you not published them so far?
Jung: Because they were not important enough. I see no particular
importance in them. (Maguire, 1974: xxx)

However, shortly after this Jung wrote to a pupil he had asked to go
through his correspondence with Freud:

> Best thanks for the quotation from that accursed correspondence. For me
> it is an unfortunately inexpungeable reminder of the incredible folly that
> filled the days of my youth. The journey from cloud-cuckoo-land back to
> reality lasted a long time. In my case Pilgrim's Progress consisted in my
> having to climb down a thousand ladders until I could reach out my hand
> to the little clod of earth that I am. (Maguire, 1974: xxx)

There was a great deal of negotiation before agreement was reached
between the Freud and Jung families to publish. Finally, on 25
February 1970, Jung's son, Franz, flew from Zürich to London with
the original Freud letters to meet with Freud's son, Ernst, at the
latter's home in St. John's Wood. The two got on well and had
much in common as they were both architects.

A cross-section of the correspondence will be reproduced below
to illustrate key moments of the interaction between the two men.
Freud started off by addressing Jung as 'Dear Colleague' which
changed to 'Dear Friend', while Jung out of deference as the much
younger of the two addressed Freud always as 'Dear Professor
Freud'. Even as early as 1906, Jung is writing of his doubts of the
sexual aetiology of all neuroses, as follows.

Jung (23 October 1906):

> It is possible that my reservations . . . are due to lack of experience. But
> don't you think that a number of borderline phenomena might be
> considered more appropriately in terms of the other basic drive, *hunger*:
> for instance, eating, sucking (predominantly hunger), kissing (predomi-
> nantly desexuality)? Two complexes existing at the same time are always
> bound to coalesce psychologically, so that one of them invariably
> contains constellated aspects of the other. (Maguire, 1974: 7)

Jung (24 May 1907):

> Your *Gravida* is magnificent. I gulped it at one go . . . Often I have to
> transport myself back to the time before the reformation of my
> psychological thinking to re-experience the charges that were laid against
> you. I simply can't understand them any more . . . So you may be
> absolutely right when you seek the cause of our opponents' resistance in
> affects, especially sexual affects. (Maguire, 1974: 49)

Freud (6 June 1907):

> I am very much surprised to hear that I am the rich man from whose
> table you glean a few crumbs. (Maguire, 1974: 58)

Jung (19 August 1907):

Do you regard sexuality as the mother of all feelings? Isn't sexuality for you merely one component of the personality (albeit the most important) . . . Are there not hysterical symptoms which, though co-determined by the sexual complex, are predominantly conditioned by a sublimation or by a non-sexual complex (profession, job, etc)? (Maguire, 1974: 79)

Freud (27 August 1907):

For the present I do not believe that anyone is justified in saying that sexuality is the mother of all feelings . . . I regard (for the present) the role of sexual complexes in hysteria merely as a theoretical necessity. (Maguire, 1974: 80)

Jung (28 October 1907):

Actually – and I confess this to you with a struggle – I have a boundless admiration for you both as a man and a researcher, and I bear you no conscious grudge. So the self-preservation complex does not come from there; it is rather that my veneration for you has something of the character of a 'religious' crush. Though it does not really bother me, I still feel it is disgusting and ridiculous because of its undeniable erotic undertone. This abominable feeling comes from the fact that as a boy I was the victim of a sexual assault by a man I once worshipped. (Maguire, 1974: 95)

Freud (2 January 1910):

It has occurred to me that the ultimate basis of man's need for religion is *infantile helplessness*, which is so much greater in man than in animals. After infancy he cannot conceive of a world without parents and makes for himself a just God and a kindly nature, the two worst anthropomorphic falsifications. (Maguire, 1974: 284)

Freud (3 March 1911):

Since the day before yesterday I have been the chairman of the Vienna group. It had become impossible to go on with Adler; he was quite aware of it himself and admitted that his chairmanship was incompatible with his new theories. Stekel, who now sees eye to eye with him, followed suit . . . I now feel that I must avenge the offended goddess Libido . . . I see now that Adler's seeming decisiveness concealed a good deal of confusion. I would never have expected a psychoanalyst to be so taken in by the ego. (Maguire, 1974: 400)

Freud (5 March 1912):

I have pointed out to you that the Association cannot prosper when the president loses interest in it over a period of months, especially when he has so unreliable an assistant as our friend Riklin. You seem to recognize that I am right . . . You make it clear to me that you don't wish to write to me at present, and I reply that I am trying to make the privation easy for myself . . . You speak of the need for intellectual independence and quote Nietzsche in support of your view . . . But if a third party were to read this passage, he would ask me when I had tried to tyrannize you intellectually, and I should have to say: I don't know. (Maguire, 1974: 492)

Jung (2 August 1912):

In certain circumstances, indeed as a general rule, the fantasy object is *called* 'mother'. But it seems to me highly unlikely that primitive man ever passed through an era of incest. Rather, it would appear that the first manifestation of incestuous desire was the prohibition itself. (Maguire, 1974: 512)

Jung (3 December 1912):

Our analysis, you may remember, came to a stop with your remark that you 'could not submit to analysis *without losing your authority*.' These words are engraved on my memory as a symbol of everything to come. (Maguire, 1974: 526)

Freud (5 December 1912):

For the present I can only suggest a household remedy: let each of us pay more attention to his own than to his neighbour's neurosis. (Maguire, 1974: 529)

Jung (18 December 1912):

I would, however, point out that your technique of treating your pupils like patients is a *blunder*. In that way you produce either slavish sons or impudent puppies . . . You go around sniffing out all the symptomatic actions in your vicinity, thus reducing everyone to the level of sons and daughters who blushingly admit the existence of their faults. Meanwhile you remain on top as the father, sitting pretty. (Maguire, 1974: 535)

Freud (3 January 1913):

It is a convention among us analysts that none of us need feel ashamed of his own bit of neurosis. But one who while behaving abnormally keeps shouting that he is normal gives ground for the suspicion that he lacks insight into his illness. Accordingly, I propose that we abandon our personal relations entirely. (Maguire, 1974: 539)

Jung (6 January 1913):

I accede to your wish that we abandon our personal relations, for I never thrust my friendship on anyone. You yourself are the best judge of what this moment means to you. 'The rest is silence'. (Maguire, 1974: 540)

The Break with Freud

There is an archetypal, even tragic, feel to the decline of the relationship that existed for a few years between Freud and Jung. The last time the two actually met was in September 1913 in Munich at the fourth International Psychoanalytical Congress. Jung was again put forward as president of the IPA and Freud's close followers, Abraham, Ferenczi, Jones, Rank amongst them, handed in 22 blank ballot papers. However, 52 analysts voted in favour of Jung so he was reinstated in office. Over the following months there was consternation in the Freudian camp about Jung's continuing role in the IPA and as editor of the *Yearbook* but on 29 October of that year he stood down as editor followed in April 1914 by his resignation as president of the IPA.

Jung and Bennet, in their written accounts of what led to the final rupture, cite Jung's book, *Psychology of the Unconscious*, published in 1916. The title was later changed to *Symbols of Transformation*, as Volume 5 of the *Collected Works*. While Jung was working on this book he had dreams that presaged the break with Freud but as he says in the Foreword to the fourth Swiss edition:

> The whole thing came upon me like a landslide that cannot be stopped . . . it was the explosion of all those psychic contents which could find no room, no breathing-space, in the constricting atmosphere of Freudian psychology and its narrow outlook. (Jung, 1956: xxiii)

In this work, Jung put forward his own view of libido and incest which portrayed them as having a spiritual meaning:

> Sexuality is of the greatest importance as the expression of the chthonic spirit. That spirit is the 'other face of God', the dark side of the God-image. The question of the chthonic spirit has occupied me ever since I began to delve into the world of alchemy. Basically, this interest was awakened by that early conversation with Freud, when, mystified, I felt how deeply stirred he was by the phenomenon of sexuality. (Jung, 1963: 192)

Paul Stepansky, in his paper, 'The Empiricist as Rebel: Jung, Freud and the Burdens of Discipleship', takes a very different view of both the book, *Symbols of Transformation*, and of the final cause of the parting of the ways between Jung and Freud. He starts with a close scrutiny of the supposed controversial parts of the book and concludes that these could in no way have given cause for the contentious split between the two men. The move away from a narrow formulation of the libido concept was instigated by Freud himself in his analysis of paranoia in the Schreber case history. Jung himself stated that Freud here demonstrates that the paranoiac's longing for the reality principle cannot be traced to the withdrawal of libido alone. 'Freud as well as myself, saw the need of widening this conception of libido' (Stepansky, 1992: 177).

Stepansky also points to Freud as the original source of Jung's exploration of the collective unconscious as the realm of myth-making and symbolism, for instance, in his study of Leonardo da Vinci. After reading this, Jung wrote to him in 1910:

> *Leonardo* is wonderful. The transition to mythology grows out of this essay from inner necessity, actually it is the first essay of yours with whose inner development I felt perfectly in tune from the start. (Maguire, 1974: 329)

Stepansky further suggests that: 'However extensive the classical and philological themes contained in the Miller fantasies, Miss Miller's "vision of creation" remains first and foremost a function of an "erotic impression"; the source of her symbolical productions is "an erotic conflict"' (Stepansky, 1992: 176).

Most significantly of all, he points out that in the chapter on *Symbolism of the Mother and Rebirth*, Jung's hypothesis that incestuous desire signifies the wish to return to the mother in order to be re-born is similar in kind to Freud's concept of 'primal narcissism'. As early as 1910, the latter had given his blessing to an early draft of the work.

Stepansky's aim in revising this account of the Freud/Jung split is to pave the way for his own hypothesis about what took place. He questions why Freud, for whom the sexual aetiology of neuroses was the central tenet of psychoanalysis, would have named 'as his heir apparent a disciple whose ruthless empiricism undercut the social and clinical crusade that was already under way?' (Stepansky, 1992: 187).

In a letter of 1908 responding to his Berlin disciple, Karl Abraham, Freud tries to assuage the former's qualms over Jung's silence on the sexual theory. Freud says that it is easier for Abraham to accept this as they are racial kinsmen while Jung 'as a Christian and a pastor's son finds his way to me only against great inner resistance. His association with us is the more valuable for that analysis escaped the danger of becoming a Jewish national affair' (Stepansky, 1992: 191).

Freud also pinned his hopes on Jung to take his work further in applying it to the psychoses as well as the neuroses. For these reasons:

> Freud . . . consciously deceived Jung in allowing him to believe his conditional appropriation of dream mechanics and energetics constituted full-fledged loyalty to the movement . . . The entire episode . . . is a long and ominous testimony to Freud's emotional investment in the institutionalized movement his work had created. (Stepansky, 1992: 192)

Freud's view of the rupture is different to this as he demonstrates in a scathing attack on Jung and what he terms the 'Neo-Zurich' school in his *On the History of the Psycho-Analytic Movement*. As he says there about them:

> Suppose – to make use of a simile – that in a particular social group there lives a *parvenu*, who boasts of being descended from a noble family living in another place. It is pointed out to him, however, that his parents live somewhere in the neighborhood, and that they are quite humble people. There is only one way of escape from his difficulty and he seizes on it. He can no longer repudiate his parents, but he asserts that they themselves are of noble lineage and have merely come down in the world; and he procures a family-tree from some obliging official source. It seems to me that the Swiss have been obliged to behave in much the same way . . . (i)f ethics and religion were not allowed to be sexualized but had to be something 'higher' from the start, and if nevertheless the ideas contained in them seemed undeniably to be descended from the Oedipus and family-complex . . . (Freud, 1966: 73)

Freud makes it clear that, as far as he is concerned, Jung's modification of the sexual theory represented both an abandonment of psychoanalysis and a secession from it. This was formalized in the UK when the British Medical Association (BMA) set up a committee that included Ernest Jones to investigate psychoanalysis. The BMA Report of 1928 defined psychoanalysis as 'the technique devised by Freud, who first used the term, and the theory which he has built upon his work' (King and Steiner, 1991: 12). The Report went on to recognize the distinction between 'psychoanalysts' and 'pseudo-analysts'. In this way, Jones enabled psychoanalysts to differentiate themselves from other forms of psychotherapeutic practice and to be treated like any other form of specialism in medicine.

> This was the first time an official national body of the medical profession from any country had recognized the distinction between 'psycho-analysts' and 'pseudo-analysts', as well as the qualifications established by membership of the International Psychoanalytical Association. (King and Steiner, 1991: 13)

Aftermath

The professional aftermath of the rupture between Freud and Jung was as follows. Zurich up to this point had been the second most important centre of psychoanalysis after Vienna. There was a flourishing Psychoanalytical Association which was initially attached to both the Burghölzli Hospital and the University of Zurich. In 1912 this separated from the Burghölzli and became an independent institution in its own right. In 1914, after Freud published his *On the History of the Psychoanalytic Movement*, the

Zurich Psychoanalytical Association voted to leave the International Psychoanalytic Association. This group consisted mainly of medical doctors that met regularly until 1918 when it became absorbed into the newly formed Analytical Psychology Club.

The emotional impact of the rupture on both men was profound and Jung suffered from what Ellenberger calls a 'creative illness' for a few years after the break with Freud. The background to the relationship with Freud, including the final denouement, is illuminated by the Jungian analyst, Murray Stein, in his study of Jung's problematic relationship to both his personal father and to what might be called the archetypal Father in the form of Christianity. Stein's account of Jung's childhood shows the latter's growing awareness of the ailments of Christianity and of his father's resultant withered attitude to spiritual life. As has already been mentioned, Jung senior was a pastor in the Swiss Reformed Church but, in spite of this, he was unable to help his son with his own doubts about Christian theology and doctrine. Jung was left feeling that neither was able to struggle with the great spiritual issues of the day.

> Stein's convincing argument is that Jung saw his spiritual vocation as the path to healing the source of his father's suffering. In this way, Jung's attitude to Christianity was akin to a patient who needed 'treatment'. (Casement, 1998: 73)

The main thrust of Stein's thesis is that Jung experienced his father as being content to go along with a conventional view of the all-good Christian God with the consequence that he never had the courage to experience God's dark or shadow side. 'This made his religion shallow . . . and in the end, Jung felt, "faith broke faith with him"' (Stein, 1985: 74).

The encounter with Freud was to a greater or lesser extent fuelled by a wish-fulfilment for the idealized father, one who had the courage to face the dark side of life. As the idealization began to break down and Jung experienced Freud as one-sided and dogmatic, his father complex resurfaced with renewed energy as he tried to 'redeem' Freud from the error of his ways. Michael Fordham, the eminent English Jungian analyst, in the account he wrote of his own life, describes his last meeting with Jung shortly before the latter's death in 1961. Jung had written a letter to an English colleague saying that he had failed in his mission and was misunderstood and misrepresented. Fordham visited him in an effort to ease his distress but ends by saying: 'When I came to see him I did not touch on these matters but spoke superficially. If I had not done that I would have had to convey my thought that it was the delusion of being a world saviour that made him feel a failure' (Fordham, 1993: 120).

All of which helps to explain the strength of feeling he expresses in the final written communications with Freud and in subsequent publications. In 1958 he published *Answer to Job*, his own account of the confrontation between the Hebrew God, Yahweh and his disciple, Job. For Jung, Yahweh is a being consumed with his own omniscience and omnipotence and finally has to acknowledge the superior integrity of Job, who manages to remain true to his own faith in the face of Yahweh's onslaughts. The following quote is ostensibly written about the latter but it could equally apply to Freud:

> With his touchiness and suspiciousness the mere possibility of doubt was enough to infuriate him and induce that peculiar double-faced behaviour of which he had already given proof in the Garden of Eden, when he pointed out the tree to the First Parents and at the same time forbade them to eat of it. In this way he precipitated the Fall, which he apparently never intended. (Jung, 1958: 13)

Creative Illness

From 1913 until 1918 Jung experienced what he called a period of confrontation with the unconscious when he had apocalyptic dreams and visions.

> After the parting of the ways with Freud, a period of inner uncertainty began for me. It would be no exaggeration to call it a state of disorientation. I felt totally suspended in mid-air, for I had not yet found my own footing. (Jung, 1963b: 194)

> I lived as if under constant inner pressure. At times this became so strong that I suspected there was some psychic disturbance in myself. (Jung, 1963b: 197)

He felt the need to return to childhood and began to play childish games building houses and villages with stones. He found that this contact with stone helped to connect him to his fantasies and creativity. In the autumn of 1913 he had an overpowering vision in the course of which he saw a monstrous flood covering the northern and low-lying lands between the North Sea and the Alps. As it approached Switzerland, the mountains grew higher to protect the country from the mighty yellow waves in which floated the rubble of civilizations and the bodies of thousands of people. Then the whole sea turned to blood. At the time he thought that this indicated that he was menaced by an approaching psychosis and did not think of war at all.

Towards the end of 1913 he had the following dream:

> I was with an unknown, brown-skinned man, a savage, in a lonely, rocky mountain landscape. It was before dawn; the eastern sky was already bright, and the stars fading. Then I heard Siegfried's horn sounding over the mountains and I knew that we had to kill him. We were armed with rifles and lay in wait for him on a narrow path over the rocks. Then Siegfried appeared high up on the crest of the mountain, in the first ray of the rising sun. On a chariot made of the bones of the dead he drove at a furious speed down the precipitous slope. When he turned a corner, we shot at him, and he plunged down, struck dead. (Jung, 1963b: 204)

Jung pondered for a long time on this dream before its meaning began to dawn. His initial reaction had been remorse and disgust that he had killed something so great and beautiful. Then he realized that Siegfried represented the Teutonic wish to impose their will heroically on the world. This had also been true of himself but he began to see that that was no longer what suited him and that the heroic attitude that Siegfried personified had to be 'killed'.

In abandoning the heroic attitude which may also be equated with consciousness, Jung let himself experience the depths of the psyche, in the course of which he encountered many figures that impressed him and made him realize that there were things in his psyche that he did not produce but which had a life of their own. One such personification he named Philemon, a wise-old-man figure. It was from Philemon that Jung learned about the *objective psyche* which is different from the personal unconscious. He also represented for Jung superior insight and became almost like a living personality with whom Jung would walk in the garden.

> It is, of course, ironical that I, a psychiatrist, should at almost every step of my experiment have run into the same psychic material which is the stuff of psychosis and is found in the insane. This is the fund of unconscious images which fatally confuse the mental patient. But it is also the matrix of a mythopoeic imagination which has vanished from our rational age. (Jung, 1963b: 213)

What Jung also encountered in the years 1916–18 was what he came to see as the bedrock of psychological wholeness, that which both keeps the psyche from falling apart at times of great stress but also transcends and goes beyond the psyche. He termed this the '*self*', which he began to express in circular drawings or mandalas. As a result of this, he realized that the goal of psychic development is the self and that this comes about as a result of the circumnamulation of the self that lies at the centre of the individual. This will be elaborated later in the book.

Women in Jung's Life

What Jung claims kept him sane at the time of his 'creative illness' was his family and his work. He first saw his future wife, Emma Rauschenbach, when he was 21 and she was 14. She came from an affluent family of watchmakers whose lifestyle contrasted greatly with Jung's impoverished background. They met again when he was 27 and she 20, were married in 1903 and had four daughters and a son over the next few years. Their first married home was a flat above Eugen Bleuler and his wife at the Burghölzli Hospital. In the meantime, a house was being built for them at Küsnacht, a village on the side of the lake at Zurich.

The marriage lasted for 52 years until Emma's death in 1955 by which he was deeply moved, telling Michael Fordham at the funeral that she was a queen. There is no doubt that Emma Jung was the most important woman in Jung's life. She had a mind of her own as well as being psychologically minded and, unlike Jung, she was interested in the personal lives of individual patients and their environment. Although she wrote little in her own right, Emma contributed more than any of the other women in Jung's life to his ideas, for instance, in giving the *animus* the positive aspect as a woman's logos that it lacked before.

Despite his own happy marriage, Jung appears to have had little respect for the conventions of marriage and parenthood, as shown by a remark of his that is on record made at a meeting in Vienna 1931: 'There are few things which have caused as much anxiety, unhappiness, and evil as the compulsion to give birth' (Adler, 1976: 15). Emma Jung feared that her pregnancies would turn Jung away from her.

For his part, Jung wrote a paper on marriage in 1925 called 'Marriage as a Psychological Relationship', in which he talked about one partner in the relationship being the 'container' and the other the 'contained'. By this he meant that the contained – that is, the simpler personality – finds everything they need within the marriage, whilst the container – the more complex one – becomes increasingly frustrated and seeks fulfilment elsewhere. If this remains unresolved between the two it can lead either to the breakdown of the marital relationship or to an increasingly collusive state of affairs.

On the whole, Jung's written accounts of external marriage are tinged with a negative aspect and he always expressed a bias in favour of individual development versus the mutual understanding that may come out of the marital relationship. This balance was redressed by the Jungian analyst, Guggenbühl-Craig, who wrote in 1977 an account called *Marriage – Dead or Alive?*, of how people can develop as individuals within the kind of marriage that serves the deepest interests of both.

For Jung, it was the higher marriage or *hierosgamos* signifying an internal connection that fascinated him. This was represented by the archetypal union in the rebirth mysteries of antiquity, in the symbolic marriage of Christ and the Church and in the alchemical conjunction of sun and moon. The higher or sacred marriage may lead to the birth of the divine child. This will be elaborated in a later chapter on the alchemical container of analysis and the symbolic 'marriage' of analyst and analysand.

Jung's attitude to women appears to have been ambivalent. On the one hand, he seems to have needed an anima figure or *femme inspiratrice* with whom to have 'poetry'. However, he also called them 'animus hounds' a particularly damning expression he used for any woman that he found opinionated or overpowering.

There was also the group of women analysts and colleagues who were gathered around Jung in Zurich, some of whom remained unmarried and instead devoted their lives to working with his ideas. The most prominent amongst these were Marie-Louise von Franz, the daughter of an Austrian nobleman, and Barbara Hannah, the Dean of Chichester's daughter. The Jungian analyst, Thomas Kirsch, the son of a close collaborator of Jung's, James Kirsch, has written a book, *The Jungians*, chronicling the development of the Jungian world. In this he states that von Franz was the person who carried on Jung's legacy and that her position to Jung may be compared to Anna Freud's to Freud.

Another woman devotee of Jung's was Yolande Jacobi, a Hungarian Jewess married to a prominent lawyer, who managed to escape from Vienna after the *Anschluss* – the union of the Austrian Republic and the German Reich in 1938. All three of these women were prolific writers.

Jung visited the USA again in 1912, this time without Freud. In the course of this visit, he associated with some of the wealthiest American families and became acquainted with Edith Rockefeller, the daughter of John D. Rockefeller, the founder of Standard Oil Trust. She married Harold Fowler McCormick, another wealthy American. Edith McCormick suffered from agoraphobia and she offered to set Jung up in practice in the USA in order that he could treat her. Instead, he suggested she come to Zurich, which she did in 1913. It was the McCormick money that funded the first Psychological Club in Zurich. This was the prototype of many Analytical Psychology Clubs that flowered in other parts of the world that preceded the formal establishment of training institutes.

Another key woman in this context was Aniela Jaffé, mentioned above as the co-author with Jung of *Memories, Dreams, Reflections*. She started analysis with him in 1937, became the secretary of the Jung Institute in Zurich in 1947 and subsequently Jung's own secretary.

Femmes Inspiratrices

There was a line of inspiring women in Jung's life, starting with his cousin, Hélène Preiswerk, who had mediumistic gifts and to whom he dedicated his doctoral thesis.

Another was Frank Miller, an American patient of the Swiss–French psychiatrist, Théodore Flournoy. Sonu Shamdasani says of her: 'A feminine icon stands at the head of Jung's *Transformations and Symbols of the Libido*, presiding over the birth of Analytical Psychology' (Shamdasani, 1990: 26). This is the book that has been cited as leading to the final rupture with Freud in 1913. The main theme of the book is the heroic struggle for deliverance from the Mother so that the individual who achieves autonomy is the one who is born twice – once physically and the second time symbolically. Frank Miller, like Jung, was given to mythological fantasies and this is what struck a deep chord in him when he read the case history that Flournoy sent him. It released in Jung the fantasies that he felt had been bottled up during the years with Freud.

The material that Miller produced was in the form of fantasies and active imagination rather than having its origins in childhood and this was to become Jung's own approach. It led him to conceptualize that there are two forms of thinking: directed and fantasy. The former he viewed as culturally formed by education, which transformed it from the subjective, individual sphere to the objective, social sphere. The second was effortless and spontaneous and guided by unconscious motives. This was a crucial landmark in Jung's development and everything he wrote since that time was informed by this duality.

In his paper on Frank Miller, Shamdasani also points to the enormous impact Flournoy had on Jung's work, which he claims was at least as great as Freud's. Some of these influences include the autonomy of the psyche; teleology based on Aristotle's doctrine of final causes; the compensatory nature of the unconscious and synchronicity. In his *From India to the Planet Mars*, Flournoy showed 'the ancestral and extraterrestrial existences of his medium, who he dubbed Hélène Smith, to be the work of the subconscious creative imagination fueled by cryptomnesias' (Shamdasani, 1990: 39).

Sabina Spielrein

Another inspiring woman in Jung's life was the young Russian Jewess, Sabina Spielrein. She was admitted as an inpatient to the Burghölzli in August 1904 diagnosed as suffering from psychotic hysteria and became Jung's first psychoanalytic patient. He treated her intensively with this method for two months, using Janet's method of sitting behind the patient. Her presenting symptom was that she oscillated between masturbating and bouts of self-disgust; this appeared to be associated to fantasies of being beaten by her father which produced in her erotic feelings followed by a sense of disgust with herself.

Jung quickly became aware that she was unusually bright and treated her both psychoanalytically as well as didactically, giving her his doctoral dissertation to read. In 1905, she was well enough to enrol as a medical student at the University of Zurich. There are two accounts of this lengthy relationship, which later included Freud, to whom Jung turned for help when he felt out of his depth. The first account was written in 1984 by the Jungian analyst, Aldo Carotenuto, which maintains a neutral position on whether Jung and Spielrein actually had a physical affair (Carotenuto, 1984). She certainly seemed to want a soulful union with Jung, which would give birth to a creative idea that she conceptualized as a symbolic son (whom she called 'Siegfried').

The other, later account by John Kerr, the American clinical psychologist and historian, is entitled *A Most Dangerous Method*. Kerr is in no doubt that the two consummated their love in an erotic relationship but he also rehabilitates Spielrein as a significant contributor to psychoanalytic thinking in areas such as repression, schizophrenia and the death-wish (Kerr, 1994).

Although Carotenuto appears uncertain as to the full extent of the relationship between Spielrein and Jung, he acknowledges that they were erotically involved and that Jung's letters about the matter to Freud in 1908 are fearful and guilt-ridden. Freud rallied around Jung and Carotenuto is critical of the two men's attitude to Sabina. For instance, Freud writes to Jung in 1909: 'The way these women manage to charm us with every conceivable psychic perfection until they have attained their purpose is one of nature's greatest spectacles' (Carotenuto, 1982: 175).

In contrast, Carotenuto says that her letters to Freud, starting in 1909, display dignity and a sense of responsibility: 'So my last hope of salvation was to speak with a person who deeply loves and respects him (Jung), who possesses a profound knowledge of human nature, and when I received your last letter, unfavorable though it was to me, tears came to my eyes: "He loves him! What if he could understand all this!"' (Carotenuto, 1984: 176).

The two – Jung and Spielrein – suffered all the bitter-sweet torments that are the inevitable accompaniments to passion: ecstasy, jealousy, anguish. Jung, for his part, feared exposure and ruin and tried in vain to separate from Spielrein. When her mother wrote a pleading letter to Jung asking him not to undo the good work he had done by exceeding the bounds of friendship, he replied:

> You do understand, of course, that a man and a girl cannot possibly continue indefinitely to have friendly dealings with one another without the likelihood that something more may enter the relationship. For what would restrain the two from drawing the consequences of their love? A *doctor* and his *patient*, on the other hand, can talk of the most intimate matters for as long as they like, and the patient may expect her doctor to give her all the love and concern she requires. But the doctor knows his limits and will never cross them, for he is *paid* for his trouble . . . if you wish me to adhere strictly to my role as doctor, you should pay me a fee as suitable recompense for my trouble. (Carotenuto, 1984: 94)

Spielrein sent this to Freud with an accompanying letter, as follows:

> How terribly insulting that must have been for my mother . . . though my mother did not know that Dr. Jung had the right to accept private patients, she did give him gifts in lieu of money . . . the entire matter has become complicated lately (precisely because he has ceased to figure as a doctor in my life). (Carotenuto, 1984: 95)

As more letters between the protagonists have come to light, recent scholarship has taken an increasingly nuanced view of the most famous triangle in psychoanalysis. Zvi Lothane's (1999) paper in the *International Journal of Psychoanalysis* divides the relations between Jung and Speilrien from 1904–1911 into four phases: 1904–5 – the inpatient treatment; 1906–8 – the deepening friendship; 1909–10 – the erotic/sensual relationship; 1911 – Jung published her doctoral dissertation in the *Jahrbuch*.

Lothane dissents from the view that the relationship between Spielrein and Jung in the years between 1904–10 was a sexual one and an ethical breach of the doctor–patient boundary. Jung appears to have misinterpreted rumours concerning a sexual scandal to do with another woman as emanating from Spielrein and Lothane's conclusion is that the episode had no ill effect on the Freud/Jung relationship. In an unpublished letter of Spielrein's written in 1908 to her mother she declares:

> So far we have remained at the level of poetry that is not dangerous, and we shall remain at that level, perhaps until the time when I will become a doctor. (Lothane, 1999: 1197)

Lothane interprets the much-discussed term 'poetry' in this letter as pointing to tender embraces, as the letter makes it clear that she and Jung have not consummated a sexual relationship. Freud is even-handed in his interpretation of both Spielrein and Jung being caught in 'endopsychic' phenomena and confesses that he himself has come close to it a number of times. According to Lothane, Freud's letter of 1909 about the woman patient who had introduced herself to a colleague as Jung's mistress refers to another woman entirely.

Sabina eventually moved to Vienna where she trained to be a psychoanalyst. She moved to Geneva in the 1920s, where she was a member of the Psychoanalytic Society along with Piaget (whom she analysed) and de Saussure. She returned to Russia in 1923 and was shot with both her daughters by the Nazis in 1941.

Perhaps her greatest legacy for Jung was the insight into the erotic transference/countertransference they experienced together, which he later wrote up as *The Psychology of the Transference*. Her paper 'Destruction as the cause of Coming into Being', prefigures Freud's theory of the *death instinct* which he expounds in *Beyond the Pleasure Principle*, and in which he acknowledges his debt to Spielrein.

Another woman who was intimately involved with Jung and with the first Psychological Club founded in Zurich in 1916 was a Dutchwoman, Maria Moltzer. According to his close associate, Jolande Jacobi, Jung had an affair with Moltzer.

Toni Wolff

The most long-lasting extra-marital relationship of Jung's was with Toni Wolff, a young woman in her twenties when he first met her, who came from a wealthy Swiss family. She was initially a patient of his whom he treated for depression. Later, when Jung struggled with the psychotic images that arose from the depths of his unconscious after the break with Freud, it was Toni who was his guide and who helped him through the difficult years. In the following quote '*nekyia*' refers to Odysseus's return from the land of the dead in the *Odyssey*.

> When Jung began his *nekyia* into the unconscious, Toni Wolff was the one he turned to. He shared his dreams and active imaginations with her, which he recorded in his Red Book. She became his soul mate for psychological matters in a way that Emma could not provide. (Kirsch, 2000: 8)

She was a gifted analyst and helped Jung with his work in every way becoming a founding member of the Psychological Club in Zurich in 1916 and its president from 1928 to 1945. For much of that time, individuals who entered analysis with Jung would also have analysis with Toni Wolff.

A triangular relationship existed between Emma, Toni and Jung for forty years but their relationship had cooled by the end of the 1940s and he did not attend her funeral after her sudden death in 1953. Gerhard Adler had an analytic session with her on the day before she died, which he described as follows:

> I could tell her how I felt that all the splintered bits of my psyche seemed to have come together, how conscious and unconscious, female and male aspects, felt in a true *coniunctio*. It was one of those rare hours, when everything seemed 'in Tao'. Toni was so near and warm and human, with a charming smile – we laughed a lot during this hour – that our relationship seemed closer than ever. (Adler, 1978: 11)

Adler was brought to this final, fateful meeting with Toni Wolff through a series of synchronistic happenings. Jung's concept of synchronicity is described by Adler as follows:

> . . . the concept of a space-time-continuum . . . explains synchronistic phenomena as well as the knowledge of future or spatially distant events . . . Here we are in the realm of transcendental phenomena, in the realm of absolute knowledge not mediated by the sense organs. The space-time-continuum of modern physics is irrepresentable just as archetypes and synchronicity produce a picture of the world so irrepresentable as to be completely baffling. (Adler, 1978: 13)

Robert Hinshaw's collection of papers on Toni Wolff, *Essays on Jung's Psychology* (2000), will shortly be available in English.

Subjective confession

This chapter has attempted to show the major personal formative encounters in Jung's life and work. His relationship to his parents was crucial in forming him both as an individual and in his ideas. As a young man, one of his influential experiences was with the occult through his mediumistic cousin, Hélène Preiswerk. A number of women after this featured prominently in his life either as co-workers and/or personal relationships. There were also several significant men, perhaps the most important being C.A. Meier, who for many years was Jung's 'crown prince' and the first president of the Jung Institute in Zurich. Other important male figures included Gerhard Adler, Peter Baynes, James Hillman, James Kirsch, Erich Neumann, Franz Riklin and Father Victor White, some of whose ideas are to be found in this book. Jung seems to have considered Neumann the most brilliant of them and the one who would continue his work – which inspired a great deal of envy from some of the other analysts around Jung.

Part of this chapter has been devoted to the controversial impact on Jung by Freud. In the volume of his works devoted to Freud and psychoanalysis, Jung states that the modern psychologist cannot make statements about the nature of the psyche that are 'true' or 'correct' but can only formulate statements that are the truest expression of their personal psychologies. Even when dealing with empirical data, the psychologist is necessarily speaking about him or herself. For Jung, Freud could not get beyond his own psychological state which was neurotic and one-sided.

The subjective nature of psychology is summarized by Jung as follows: 'Philosophical criticism has helped me to see that every psychology – my own included – has the character of a subjective confession' (Jung, 1961: 336). Here Jung demonstrates that he is an existential thinker, viz. one who draws his entire existence into his philosophical reflections. Further, this confession, with its overtones of a religious nature, was well-suited to his own approach which grew largely out of himself as *homo religiosus* for whom the meaning of life was of supreme importance.

2

Jung's Major Theoretical Contributions

There were a myriad formative encounters in Jung's life, some of which have already been delineated in the foregoing chapter. These also played an important part in the development of his theoretical formulations. Jung was a complex man who immersed himself in a great many disciplines and it is beyond the scope of this book to deal with all of them. As a result, a selective choice has been made as to which to include. Two of the most important were medicine, particularly psychiatry and psychology and have already been dealt with in the first chapter.

Another important formative discipline was philosophy. Hand in glove with this, he also turned to more esoteric sources, such as Jewish Kabbala, gnosticism, manichaeism and alchemy. The previous chapter pointed to Jung's deep-seated disillusionment, starting in youth with orthodox Christianity as practised and preached by his father, Pastor Jung. This upheld the doctrine of the all-good, all-perfect God alienating both the divine and humankind from its own darker side and hence from a sense of its own completeness. In spite of this, Jung remained a life-long Protestant but became increasingly interested in esoteric religions.

Jung's turning to other religions and mysteries represented his quest for the wholeness that incorporating the dark or *shadow* side of the Godhead could bring about. Alchemy, for instance, could be seen as a subversive force running counter to the arid and sexless Christian doctrine of the middle ages akin to the effect psychoanalysis had on prudish Victorian attitudes to sexuality. Jung was seeking not so much for another faith to substitute for Christianity but for the reality of the psyche that he felt could not be found in its teachings. 'My Christian faith had been relativized by my encounter with Eastern religions and Greek philosophy' (Jung, 1977: 213).

The early part of this chapter will look at some of the formative encounters from philosophy and religion on his ideas, starting with philosophy. He had a lifelong love/hate relationship with the latter claiming always that he was an empiricist who relied for his theorizing on the evidence of inner experience. His ambivalence towards philosophy was part of a general feeling in psychology in the late nineteenth century as it struggled to separate itself from philosophy and become a discipline in its own right. However, as a result of having their roots in philosophy, the early psychologists could not help being philosophers and Jung, in spite of his ambivalence, always acknowledged his debt to philosophy in general and to certain philosophers – described below – in particular.

Philosophy

Jung and Antiquity

In examing Jung's contributions to theory it is important to explore the roots of his epistemological theory, the study of what we know and how we know it. The first thinker, chronologically speaking, to strike a chord with Jung was the pre-Socratic Heraclitus. He was Jung's favourite Greek philosopher and is the precursor of many of his seminal theories, such as the concept of opposites and of *enantiadromia*, a psychological law which denotes 'running contrariwise' so that eventually everything turns into its opposite. Heraclitus also posited that all things are in a state of flux, which has links to the concept of process. A saying that encapsulates this is that one can never step in the same river twice.

Plato

Plato was impressed by the idea that the whole of the sensory world is ever-changing and unstable and this was to lead to one of his most important philosophical concepts: the theory of forms. Plato attempted to define the essence of reality by stating that every object that exists is an imperfect replica of an ideal form. Further, human concepts such as truth, love, beauty also have their ideal forms. By way of the dialogues, Socrates was attempting to arrive at discovering absolute truth, love and beauty, which were called virtues by Plato. The goal of human existence was the development of virtue.

Archetypal theory traces its line of descent from the theory of ideal forms. In the same way that the forms themselves are unknowable, so too are archetypes – one can only infer their existence from the manifestation of archetypal images. It is the ideal forms and the *archetypes* that they engender that emerge into consciousness. 'In Plato an extraordinarily high value is set on the archetypes as metaphysical ideas, as "paradigms" or models, while real things are held to be only the copies of these model ideas' (Jung, 1960b: 135).

The method of discourse that Socrates used in the dialogues was known as the *dialectic* – one important conception of it being that it progresses by way of 'successive corrections of an initial onesidedness by means of a series of compensations and modifications aiming at some synthesis that is more comprehensive, larger' (Jarrett, 1992: 15). The psyche's propensity for compensation of any one-sided attitude is a central concept of Jung's as is the dialectic that exists between analyst and analysand in a Jungian analysis.

For both Plato and Jung the essential human quest lay in solving moral and religious problems.

Aristotle

From Aristotle, Plato's student, Jung derived the all-important category of *teleology*: the doctrine of final causes. In Aristotle's philosophy, this was an extension of Plato's theory of forms which provided the blueprint that guides the object to its final state or *telos*. The object may never achieve its ideal because of impediments in the way but, according to Aristotle, all life – including that of human beings – has inborn goals. The underlying pattern that is there in Aristotle's teleology is repeated in Jung's view of the individuation process.

In this way it is possible to see Platonic and Aristotelian ideas as formative of Jung's thinking as they are, of course, of European thought in general.

Jung and the Enlightenment

The leitmotif of Jung's life can be seen running through from his early to his late publications. In 1895, at the beginning of his first year at university, he joined a fraternity, Zofingia and over the next few years delivered five lectures which came to be known as the Zofingia lectures. In the first, 'The Border Zones of Exact Sciences', delivered in 1896, he upheld the vitalistic view of life which claims that knowing and purpose are present in life itself against a mechanistic view that sets limits to knowledge and a science that reduces reality to matter. The proponents of the latter approach were thinkers like Hermann von Helmholtz, the discoverer of the laws of thermodynamics, and Emil Du Bois-Reymond. The latter distinguished between things that can be known and things which will never be known.

Jung profoundly disagreed with this mechanistic view and in these early student lectures may be seen the beginnings of his future theory of knowledge. The main emphasis for him lies in *experience*, which centres on religious experience based on inner reality deeply felt not on rational or dogmatic theory. An earlier religious thinker, Soren Kierkegaard, came to precisely the same conclusion in rejecting Hegel (Casement, 1998). It is through the acknowledgement of personal experience that the individual comes to true self-knowledge and to the transcendent centre of his being, which Jung later called the *Self*. Both Kierkegaard and Jung rejected Hegel for being too collective and focused too much on the outer world in his thinking. They concentrated instead on 'inner experience' as the all-important guide to living an ethical life.

In his third Zofingia lecture Jung made the following statement, which gives the underlying basis for his theory of knowledge as personal experience.

> It is the gratification of two *a priori* requirements – the categorical imperative and the category of causality – that, under certain circumstances, makes a person happy and gives him a feeling of contentment which no external factor can confer. The frail and transitory nature of all the external factors in human life is so apparent that there is no need to discuss it . . . The only true basis for philosophy is what we experience of ourselves and, through ourselves, of the world around us. (Nagy, 1991: 18)

Here we see the profound effect of Kant on Jung's thinking that it is only through experiencing the inner moral law that humans can achieve happiness. Kant spoke of two things that fill the mind with awe: the starry heaven above and the moral law within. It is to thinkers who offer support for this point of view that Jung turns over and over again throughout his life but the first philosopher to inspire these thoughts in him was Kant. Jung's reworking of Kant was to result in his assertion that although we cannot *know* God we can observe the psychic origins of belief in God. Jung substituted 'inner experience' for Kant's *a priori* reason but both thinkers were pointing to an innate capacity in humans for knowing.

A further connection between Jung and Kant's theory of knowledge was in acknowledging the limitations of human cognitive processes. For Kant, this meant that knowledge was divided into that which one could know through cognition and which he called the phenomenal world, and that which could not, which he termed the noumenal world. This latter he also called the 'thing-in-itself' which came to have great importance for Jung in the development of his theory of archetypes. 'Things-in-themselves', according to Kant, are timeless, spaceless, causeless entities within and without the psyche. Jung experienced this theory as one of the great revelations in his life and he remained, in many ways, always a Kantian.

A critique of Jung's Kantianism is made by Marilyn Nagy, the Analytical Psychologist, and Heward Wilkinson, the Integrative

Psychotherapist. Both Nietzsche and Jung first came to Kant through Schopenhauer but the former later rejected Schopenhauer's view of Kant whereas Jung did not. As Wilkinson puts it, in his view of Kant, Jung could claim that insight through psychological process makes no *objective* claim to knowledge. But, according to Kantian logic, nobody else is in any better position to know – yet no one doubts that Newtonian physics is knowledge of *something* (personal communication with Heward Wilkinson).

Kant's epistemology is akin to Descartes in separating the subject and object of knowledge. Hegel takes on this duality but sought a third position that would reconcile the two and overcome the split between them. The Hegelian dialectic states that analysis (taking apart) is inevitably followed by synthesis (coming together). Both Hegel and Jung reached similar conclusions in reconciling the Cartesian dualism by referring to the objectivity of the subjective. In this way, the Jungian dialectic has a close affinity to the Hegelian, which is evidenced in the part of this book that deals with the *alchemical* dialectic. However, as stated above, Jung was reluctant to be associated with Hegel because of his worldliness and idealistic rationality, which Jung thought was dogmatic and lacking in an empirical basis. Further, by affirming that purposefulness in nature points to a purposeful creator, Hegel opened up a new way of theorizing about teleology – his concept of 'World Soul' bears a remarkable resemblance to Jung's 'Universal Psyche'. Hegel's 'Absolute Mind' was, to all intents and purposes, the mind of God.

Jung and Schopenhauer

The following statement by Jung shows the supreme importance of two philosophers for him: 'Mentally my greatest adventure had been the study of Kant and Schopenhauer' (Jung, 1977: 213). In *The World as Will and Idea*, Schopenhauer describes the blind will that is at the core of every being – that which Jung would have had him call 'God'. But Schopenhauer, who was not a theist, was describing his philosophy in the title which may be summarized as noumena and phenomena à la Kant, or unconscious and consciousness according to Jung. In describing archetypes, Jung insisted that these are not *ideas* in the sense of representations in the unconscious. Schopenhauer puts it thus:

> But ordinarily it is in the obscure depths of the mind that the rumination of the materials received from without takes place, through which they are worked up into thoughts; and it goes on almost as unconsciously as the conversion of nourishment into the humours and substance of the

body. Hence it is that we can often give no account of the origin of our deepest thoughts. They are the birth of our mysterious inner life. Judgements, thoughts, purposes, rise from out that deep unexpectedly and to our own surprise . . . Consciousness is the mere surface of our mind, of which as of the earth, we do not know the inside, but only the crust. (Schopenhauer, 1883: 328)

There are many other important ideas in Schopenhauer that are to be found in Jung's work, such as the following: everything that is fundamental in humans works unconsciously like a natural force; the assertion that evil is not just the privation of good but an entity in its own right; the idea that if only one individual were left in the world that one would possess the whole self-being of the world undiminished; that from the age of 36 onwards, energy is not renewable as it is in what Jung calls 'the first-half of life' and that the individual lives from then on as if living on his capital. Both men also held to a teleological world view and Jung clearly got his inspiration for an unconscious origin and centre of psychic life from Schopenhauer.

Jung and other Philosophers

As has already been pointed to, the philosophic successors of Kant took up in their different ways the new formulations of teleology opened up by him. Schelling, who labelled it the unconscious Idea, led the Romantic philosophers in pointing to the realization of this through intuition, feeling and imagination.

Eduard von Hartmann in the late nineteenth century, brought together Schopenhauer's *Will* and Schelling's unconscious *Idea* in a statistical analysis that resulted in a strong case being made for a divine order at work in nature. His major work, *The Philosophy of the Unconscious*, owed its influence to the fact that it reconciled science and God. What he was trying to achieve in marrying Schopenhauer to Schelling may be seen in the following quote:

It does not occur to . . . (Schopenhauer) to bring forward the *Idea* to explain the adaptation of means to end in Nature, which rather in genuine idealistic fashion he regards as a merely subjective appearance . . . He altogether fails to perceive that the unconscious Will of Nature *eo ipso* pre-supposes an unconscious Idea as goal, content, or object of itself, without which it would be empty, indefinite, and objectless. (Nagy, 1991: 235)

It is in our own conscious mental activity that we can gain insight into the real nature of causality as follows: an end is willed mentally followed by a conception of how it may be attained by the steps needed to realize it before reaching the desired end. In this way, final causation or teleology, is intrinsic to causality so that science needs only to include ideal (mental) states within its framework. Jung is in a direct line of descent of this kind of nineteenth century attempt to reconcile science and religion.

Another thinker whose work was dedicated to this reconciliation was Gustav Theodor Fechner, whose main philosophical conviction remained always the unity of the entire universe. For Fechner, the universe is contained in and *is* the living God. His *Elements of Psychophysics* attempted to apply physical laws to the workings of the mind. Freud was enormously influenced by Fechner's ideas on the pleasure-unpleasure principle; psychic energy; and the economic, dynamic and topographical concepts of the mind. Fechner was a pioneer in establishing psychology as a scientific discipline.

A philosopher of the early eighteenth century, C.G. Carus, also sought after a greater wholeness in examining the processes at work in nature, the body and the psyche. In the following quote Jung traces the origins of psychoanalysis and analytical psychology back many centuries through the history of ideas:

> Freud is borne along by a particular current of thought which can be traced back to the Reformation. Gradually it freed itself from innumerable veils and disguises, and it is now turning into the kind of psychology which Nietzsche foresaw with prophetic insight – the discovery of the psyche as a new fact. Some day we shall be able to see by what tortuous paths modern psychology has made its way from the dingy laboratories of the alchemists, via mesmerism and magnetism . . . to the philosophical anticipations of Schopenhauer, Carus, and von Hartmann; and how . . . it finally reached Freud through the teachings of the French hypnotists. (Jung, 1961: 325)

Carus precedes Jung in much of his thinking, for instance, in stating that the highest human fulfilment is the transition from consciousness to the unconscious. This parallels Jung's idea of becoming unconscious in the right way. Also, Carus's claim that the unconscious is affected by all humanity, as well as the life of the earth and of the world, could be substituted for Jung's collective unconscious. He went on to say that the term 'unconscious' is applied to what is objectively recognized as nature. It is easy to see why Jung claimed that had Carus lived today he would undoubtedly have been a psychotherapist.

William James

Although Jung only briefly met the American philosopher and psychologist, William James, on his first visit to the USA in 1909, James was subsequently to have a significant impact on Jung through his writings. Jung was impressed by James's stress on the importance of taking into account the holistic principle in the study of human personality. Jung was further affected by James in diverging from Freud's view of libido and broadening it into his own concept of psychic energy. Jung's theory of psychological types also derives to a considerable degree from James's ideas on the difference between the 'tough'- and 'tender'-minded individual, which in Jung's re-workings became the '*extravert*' and the '*introvert*'. Further, Jung's development of the *collective unconscious* owed much to James's work on subliminal intelligence which he claimed ranged from the bestial and archaic through the visible parts of the psyche and out to the divine and transcendent.

James's study of the immediacy of religious experience as psychologically transformative played its part in the development of Jung's ideas in this area.

F.W.H. Myers

The English poet, critic, philosopher and psychical researcher was another nineteenth century pioneer in the discovery of the unconscious. Sonu Shamdasani quotes André Breton as saying:

> And in spite of the regrettable fact that so many are unacquainted with the work of F.W.H. Myers, which anteceded that of Freud, I think we owe more than is generally conceded to what William James justly called the gothic psychology of F.W.H. Myers. (Shamdasani, 1993: 101)

The discoverer of automatic writing unleashed as big a storm of disapproval and outrage as did the psychoanalytic 'discovery' of the role of sexuality. For Myers 'the medium of automatic writing becomes a "psychoscope" that reveals the unseen movements of the psyche' (Shamdasani, 1993: 117). To quote Myers himself: 'Automatic writing is not a key to all the recesses of our being. But it is a key to something, and it is a key that will actually turn in the lock' (Shamdasani, 1993: 117).

Pierre Janet took his notion of the subconscious self from Myers as well as his use of automatic writing as a means of exploring the subconscious and as a therapeutic tool. As was stated above, Flournoy, in comparison to Janet, proposed the existence of non-pathological and creative aspects of the subconscious and emphasized that automatic activity was not in itself inferior to volition. Where Myers differed from previous thinkers on automatism was that he attributed it not to spirits but to subliminal origins and saw it as a form of intrapsychic communication. Jung was impressed with this approach and applied it in much of his writing.

Jung and Nietzsche

Jung was so profoundly affected by Nietzsche that references to the latter are scattered throughout the *Collected Works*. Like Jung, Nietzsche's father was also a pastor and both might be regarded as essentially psychologized Protestants. Nietzsche's ideas are the precursors of many of those in psychoanalysis, although Freud claimed not to have read him. Curiously, in the first volume of the *Collected Works*, Jung quotes a long passage from Nietzsche's *Thus Spake Zarathustra*, which is a striking example of cryptomnesia as it closely replicates an entry in a ship's log that Nietzsche would have had access to when young.

Later in Volume 1, Jung goes on to claim that Nietzsche was in the grip of an *archetype* when he wrote *Zarathustra*, as it was written at tremendous speed as if a *daimon* had erupted from his unconscious. In Nietzsche's case the daimon was Dionysus, the Greek god of wine, that he saw as the source of 'the will to power' with which he identified. According to Jung, this led to an inflation so that instead of keeping its revelations to himself Nietzsche felt he had to broadcast its message to the world. As he could not break free of the identification, he eventually suffered the fate of anyone in the grip of an archetype for any length of time, viz. the descent into madness.

Jung was particularly struck by Nietzsche's concept of the *Übermensch* which has been translated as either the *Superman* or the *Overman* – both English translations giving a misleadingly gender specific meaning to the term which is not gendered in German. Jung sensed an affinity between this and his theory of the process of *individuation*. In the years from 1934–39, he gave a series of seminars on *Zarathustra* which have been gathered together in two volumes called *Nietzsche's Zarathustra: Notes of the Seminar Given in 1934–1939 by C.G. Jung*. This was put together in 1988 by James L. Jarrett.

The importance of the *Übermensch* for Nietzsche was in overcoming all his hated dogmas of the nineteenth century: materialism, nationalism, rationality and scientific 'truths'. As was pointed out above, Jung also took on some of these in the Zofingia Lectures he wrote as a student. The following quote from Nietzsche in a recent book comparing him with Jung illustrates what he meant by the Übermensch:

> *One thing is needful*: To 'give style' to one's character – a great and rare art! It is practised by all those who survey the strengths and weaknesses of their nature and then fit them into an artistic plan until everyone of them appears as art and reason and even weaknesses delight the eye. (Hauke, 2000: 173)

Nietzsche's concept of the Übermensch was inspired by Zarathustra, the Persian prophet who had much in common with Christ. He
lived between the seventh and ninth centuries B.C. and taught that
from time to time a saviour appears bringing a new revelation.
Nietzsche's own experience of this came in his late thirties, the
transitional period from the first-half to the second-half of life. Up
to that time, he portrayed himself as the Anti-Christ incarnate
preaching anti-Christian propaganda. Through his vision of Zarathustra he brought a new message to the world that the former
Christian values were no longer enough and that a more ideal
morality was needed.

Nietzsche's *Zarathustra* was one of the first attempts in modern
times at individual initiation and his well-known cry, 'God is dead'
is the moment when he became gripped by the spirit. As Jung says:

> When you believe there is no such thing as spirit anywhere, you have
> disinfected the heavens and the whole world and found no God in it . . .
> as soon as you make such a declaration, the spirit is liberated from its
> incarnations and then it is in yourself: then your unconscious begins to
> stir. That happened to Nietzsche. His initiation process began, and he
> wrote it down as such a man would do. (Jarrett, 1992: 461)

There are parallels here with Jung's own concept of *individuation*
which points to a person's initiation into becoming wholly him or
herself distinct from others. This process is set in motion by the
stirrings in the unconscious and the activity of the self as distinct
from the ego.

This section on Nietzsche has concentrated on the link between
his concept of the Übermensch and Jung's individuation process but
there are many other shared areas in their ideas and lives. Two or
three examples will suffice to illustrate this affinity: both shared a
prophetic bent and Nietzsche, for instance, predicted the coming of
the devastating wars of the twentieth century. Both also pointed to
the declining power of Christianity as a world religion and, for
Nietzsche, Christianity encouraged a slave morality in preaching the
virtue of meekness. The opposite qualities of hardness and self-
mastery were personified by the Übermensch.

Both thinkers have also been accused of supporting the Nazi ideal
– Nietzsche with concepts such as *amor fati*, which means love of
destiny, and the *blond beast* – a term that would apply to the
ruthless man of action free to invent his own code of morality. Both
these concepts had a profound influence on Jung's ideas but were
criticized by others, such as the German philosopher, Theodor
Adorno, who, in the aftermath of Auschwitz, claimed that the
impossibility of any affirmation of life had become all too apparent.

This view is disputed, so far as Nietzsche is concerned, as follows:

> Jung retained a 'German-mythological' stance analagous to Wagner's, and from which his take on Kant did not protect him. Had he been able to learn from Nietzsche's original philosophizing and mythological psychologizing, he might have been better immunized against the mythological charisma of the Nazi seduction. (Heward Wilkinson, personal communication)

Perhaps Jung's abiding affinity with Nietzsche lay in their capacity for automomatic writing – a gift they both shared for being able to by-pass conscious processes and tap into the unconscious. This is apparent in Nietzsche's *Thus Spake Zarathustra* and *Ecce Homo* and can be seen in Jung's *Symbols of Transformation*, where he writes in the preface about 'an automatic play of ideas' or 'fantasy thinking'.

Esoteria

Jung drew his inspiration from a variety of esoteric sources, most of which reached back in time to Gnosticism, kaballah and alchemy. Others were closer in time and included three already mentioned above: William James, Frederick Myers and Theodore Flournoy.

Gnosticism

I am indebted to the scholar, Robert Segal, for much of what I am writing on the subject of Gnosticism, both here and in a later chapter with reference to Martin Buber. Segal has generously supplied me with his writings and given permission for my liberal use of them.

There are two definitions of Gnosticism. The narrow one sees it as an ancient Christian heresy that arose in the first and second century A.D. before dying out. The broad one defines it as both pre-Christian and non-Christian. Defined most broadly, Gnosticism is modern as well as ancient. Gilles Quispel, the distinguished scholar of Gnosticism, who lectured at the Jung Institute in Zurich, claims that it has its origins in the Jewish tradition.

In 1945, an Arab peasant discovered in the upper Egyptian desert near Nag Hammadi, a buried treasure consisting of two papyrus texts which showed a deep split in the early Christian Church. The texts showed that some gnostic Christians denied that Christ returned in the flesh and appointed Peter his successor; that many gnostics challenged priestly authority and believed instead in the presence of the divine within the human; and that the way to salvation was through self-knowledge. Quispel, whose admiration for

Jung was unbounded, bought the Gnostic codex, Nag Hammadi I, for Jung.

> Gnosticism . . . is the belief in an antithetical dualism of immateriality, which is good, and matter, which is evil. Gnosticism espouses radical dualism in human beings, the cosmos, and divinity; the primordial unity of all immateriality; the yearning to restore that unity; the present entrapment of a portion of immateriality in human bodies; the need for knowledge to reveal to humans that entrapment; and the dependence of humans on a savior to reveal that knowledge to them. (Segal, 1992: 3)

A great many thinkers apart from Jung have been characterized as Gnostics, including the apostle Paul, Hegel, Blake, Goethe, Byron, Nietzsche, Marx, Hesse, Heidegger, Conrad, Kerouac and Hitler. This is because they all share the 'Gnostic attitude' which may be summarized as a dissatisfaction with the world; a belief that it is possible to better it but that improvement must evolve historically; that humans can effect this change and that knowledge 'gnosis' is the key to change.

Jung was in quest of historical prefigurations for his inner experiences and he found these in Gnosticism and alchemy. He displayed an interest in both throughout his writings but considered alchemy more important and devoted three whole volumes to it. This is because he thought that Gnosticism was too distant in time to have a direct bearing on modern psychology and saw alchemy as the medieval nexus between the two.

> The experiences of the alchemists were, in a sense, my experiences, and their world was my world. This was, of course, a momentous discovery: I had stumbled upon the historical counterpart of my psychology of the unconscious. The possibility of a comparison with alchemy, and the uninterrupted intellectual chain back to Gnosticism, gave substance to my psychology. (Jung, 1963b: 231)

Gnosticism was remote for Jung because of the paucity of texts available before the Nag Hammadi discovery but Segal thinks it may also be related to the fact that, for Jung, Gnosticism was too unworldly. Alchemy, on the other hand, combines the Gnostic focus on immateriality with the modern focus on the transformation of worldly matter. For Jung, the alchemical process of extracting gold from base metals was a continuation of the Gnostic process of liberating fallen sparks from matter. Both appear outward processes but are in fact inner, psychological ones.

Jung's historical approach to the psyche points to the significance of Gnosticism for him. He saw humanity as evolving through four stages: primitive, ancient, modern and contemporary. He would have meant this schema to be taken literally to denote chronological stages of humankind's development. This kind of evolutionary/ historical approach has since been discredited so I have revised his model to apply it to psychological states rather than actual historical stages.

Briefly, the primitive stage denotes an ego that is not sufficiently distinct from both the outer world and the unconscious. Here there is little sense of individuality and Jung calls people stuck at this stage 'herd animals'. In identifying themselves with the world, primitives identify themselves with the gods they project onto it.

Ancients, for Jung, have a sturdier ego but nevertheless project themselves onto the world in the form of gods whom they worship. Like primitives, ancients experience the world through unconscious projection and are thus not differentiated from either.

Moderns possess a fully independent ego which has withdrawn projection from the world and in this way demythologized it. They are differentiated from both the outer world and the unconscious but the price they pay for that is that they are alienated from their unconscious and consider themselves to be wholly rational and scientific. The unconscious forces itself upon moderns in the form of neuroses or belief in phenomena from outer space.

Contemporaries are alive to the existence of non-rational phenomena but aware that traditional means of responding to them are dead. Contemporaries are in a minority and alone have what Jung calls a present-day consciousness. These individuals suffer from the senselessness and aimlessness of their lives and yearn for the kind of fulfilment that religion once provided and for which depth-psychology is now the only path. These are the ones who seek salvation through self-knowledge.

The link that Jung made between Gnostics and contemporaries was to see the former as erstwhile contemporaries. In this way, Jung portrays his psychology as the contemporary counterpart to Gnosticism in that Gnostics were seeking a mythology that recognized the reality of evil and the power of the feminine. They were also seeking a religion that came out of experience and not belief. These are all likewise Jungian concepts.

Jung's own Gnostic Myth: Seven Sermons to the Dead

The *Seven Sermons to the Dead* may be seen as Jung's Gnostic myth which he composed in three evenings in 1916. They sprang out of his confrontation with the collective unconscious during the five years after the break with Freud in 1912. The *Seven Sermons* are attributed to the second-century Alexandrian Gnostic Basilides but are a formulation of what Jung's unconscious figure, Philemon might have said.

The 'dead' are the poltergeists that Jung heard breaking into and occupying his house one day and were the souls of dead Christians. These had discovered that mainstream Christianity offered no answers to them after they were dead. One can see here the link to the discontent Jung felt with his father's inability to answer his questions about religious matters. In the *Seven Sermons*, one can see Jung's unconscious pressing for these answers and in this text he sees himself as a contemporary Basilides.

To summarize the *Sermons* briefly, the dead that figure in them have spent their lives in Jerusalem, the birthplace of mainstream Christianity. Basilides, on the other hand, comes from Alexandria, the meeting place of east and west. This represents Jung's ideal – the meeting of consciousness and the unconscious – so that Basilides epitomizes the individuated self. In typical Gnostic fashion, Jung's myth is a creation myth and shows ego-consciousness emerging from the pleroma, or godhead, which is the state of primordial unconsciousness. However, the *Seven Sermons* are an inverse of the usual Gnostic quest where the unconscious or godhead seeks to reveal itself to consciousness. In this text, it is unconsciousness that seeks revelation from consciousness.

Integration is the final goal of his approach and Jung's espousal of this is the key difference between himself and the Gnostics. Viewed in this way, God and the devil are both manifestations of the Gnostic *pleroma*, the state of primordial oneness, but instead of cancelling each other out they balance each other. The highest God is for Jung one that is not wholly good but evil as well. Sexuality as well as spirituality are also included in the text which again differentiates the Jungian ideal from the Gnostic. Wholeness not perfection is the aim.

The Seven Sermons prefigure what Jung is to become but is not yet and, in the texts, it is Basilides who epitomizes the individuated self. However, Jung rejects the epithet 'Gnostic' that has at times been directed at him on the grounds that he is an empirical scientist not a metaphysician. We will return to this theme later in the book when examining Martin Buber's critique of Jung.

Alchemy

Jung had a series of dreams that repeated the same theme that presaged his discovery of alchemy. The dreams showed him that beside his house stood another which was strange to him, although he knew that it had always been there. Finally he had a dream in which he reached the other house or wing and discovered a wonderful library dated from the sixteenth and seventeenth centuries. It contained a number of books full of copper engravings of a strange character and symbols that he had never seen before. Only later did he realize that they were alchemical symbols. About fifteen years later he had created a library of his like the one in the dream.

The crucial dream he had that anticipated his encounter with alchemy came to him in 1926:

> I was in the South Tyrol. It was wartime. I was on the Italian front and driving back from the front line with a little man, a peasant, in his horse-drawn wagon. All around us shells were exploding, and I knew that we had to push on as quickly as possible, for it was very dangerous.
>
> We had to cross a bridge and then go through a tunnel whose vaulting had been partially destroyed by the shells. Arriving at the end of the tunnel, we saw before us a sunny landscape, and I recognized it as the region round Verona. Below me lay the city, radiant in full sunlight. I felt relieved, and we drove on out into the green, thriving Lombard plain. The road led through lovely springtime country-side; we saw the rice fields, the olive trees, and the vineyards. Then, diagonally across the road, I caught sight of a large building, a manor house of grand proportions, rather like the palace of a North Italian duke. It was a typical manor house with many annexes and out-buildings. Just as at the Louvre, the road led through a large courtyard and past the palace. The little coach-man and myself drove in through a gate, and from here we could see, through a second gate at the far end, the sunlit landscape again. I looked round: to my right was the façade of the manor house, to my left the servants' quarters and the stables, barns, and other out-buildings, which stretched on for a long way. Just as we reached the middle of the courtyard, in front of the main entrance, something unexpected happened: with a dull clang, both gates flew shut. The peasant leaped down from his seat and exclaimed, 'Now we are caught in the seventeenth century.' Resignedly I thought, 'Well, that's that! But what is there to do about it? Now we shall be caught for years.' Then the consoling thought came to me: 'Someday, years from now, I shall get out again.' (Jung, 1963b: 228)

After this dream he ploughed through volumes of religion and philosophy but nothing helped throw light on the message of the dream. Light finally dawned in 1928 when the sinologist, Richard Wilhelm, sent Jung the text of *The Secret of the Golden Flower*, an exposition on Chinese alchemy.

> The problem of opposites called up by the shadow plays a great – indeed, the decisive – role in alchemy, since it leads in the ultimate phase of the work to the union of opposites in the archetypal form of the *hierosgamos* or 'chymical wedding'. Here the supreme opposites, male and female (as in the Chinese *yang* and *yin*), are melted into a unity purified of all opposition and therefore incorruptible. (Jung, 1953: 37)

What appealed to him in *The Secret of the Golden Flower* as he writes in his commentary on it was the parallel he discovered in the text to the psychic development of his patients. For him, the alchemical goal of extracting gold from base metals is mirrored in analytical work in the gradual extraction of the unconscious gold from the base metal of consciousness to lead to the higher union of the two. He says that the Western psyche, unlike that of the Chinese, has been uprooted from its origins in the unconscious and become one-sided. The commentary contains some of Jung's most wise quotations, as for instance when he says that the fundamental problems of life cannot be solved but simply outgrown. This is inherently so as they express the necessary polarity that exists in any self-regulating system such as the psyche is. It is remaining stuck in a problem that is pathological.

In another place he says that the one-sided consciousness of the Western psyche has led many Westerners to believe that they have outgrown gods and demons, but as he warns:

> What we have left behind are . . . not the psychic facts that were responsible for the birth of the gods. We are still as much possessed by autonomous psychic contents as if they were Olympians. Today they are called phobias, obsessions, and so forth; in a word neurotic symptoms. The gods have become diseases. (Jung, 1967: 37)

As a result of reading this text, Jung began to seek out alchemical books and found one written in 1593 called *Artis Auriferae Volumina Duo*. At first he would only look at the pictures and was so resistant to it that he left it almost untouched for two years. When he did start to read the text he still felt it was nonsense but occasionally came across a few sentences that meant something to him. Eventually he realized that the alchemists were writing in symbols that were akin to his own work on mythology and archetypes. After that he began to steep himself in alchemical texts and studied them over the next ten years.

What particularly excited Jung was the affinity he felt between his ideas and those in alchemy to do with archetypal transformation. In this way, he found the link to what Goethe was caught in his life's work on *Faust*, which Jung describes as 'a living substance, a suprapersonal process' (Jung, 1963b: 232).

Alchemy also linked him to the work of Paracelsus which finally led to him discussing it in relation to religion and psychology. As a result of this he was able to write *Psychology and Alchemy*, where he describes the alchemical process of transformation that underlay his own experiences from 1913–18. As has been said above, Jung remained a life-long Protestant and his attempt to link alchemy to Christianity ultimately led him to examine the figure of Christ as a psychological figure. In *Psychology and Alchemy*, he draws a parallel between Christ and the *lapis*, or stone, which is the central concept of the alchemists.

Jung returned to the problem of Christ in his book *Aion*, where he explores the development over the centuries of the religious content which Christ represented in the collective psyche. At that time, the power of Rome as embodied in the divine Caesar had crushed the spiritual life of countless numbers of people. Jung says that it was the Jewish concept of the Messiah that became constellated as a world issue and the Son of God, embodied in Christ, was opposed to the might of Caesar. In the technological age we live in this hope of redemption has become projected on UFOs and aliens from outer space.

Along with the religious correspondence to alchemy, Jung also explored the psychological in the form of the *transference*. This will be gone into at greater length later in this chapter with a fuller exposition of Jung's *The Psychology of the Transference*. As a preparation for that, it is important to look at how Jung came to study the concept of the *coniunctio* in alchemy. The alchemist would often use elements in his work that were oppositional because the attraction of opposites led to their eventual convergence out of which arose a new element. As so often with Jung, the move to studying this was also heralded in a dream accompanied by images of the Christ figure. As this is a long dream a summary will be given rather than a description in Jung's own words.

He dreamed once more that he was in a house with a wing he had never visited. He entered and came to a big double door which led to a room set up as a laboratory. It was his father's workroom and was full of glass bottles containing every imaginable sort of fish. As he looked round the room he noticed a curtain billowing out as if blown by a strong wind. A young man from the country materialized and Jung asked him to look and see whether a window was open. When he returned, Jung saw an expression of terror on his face. The young man said that it was haunted.

Jung then went out and found himself in his mother's room. There was no one in it but the atmosphere was uncanny. There were numbers of beds in pairs suspended from the ceiling and he knew that this was where his mother slept and that the beds were for spirits who came in pairs.

Opposite this room was a lobby with a brass band playing loudly. It was empty but the band went on blaring out dance and marching music. This was his worldly jovial façade with the mysterious rooms behind it which no one would have guessed at.

He interpreted the dream in this way and saw the most important images in the dream as the room for spirits and the fish laboratory. The former pointed for Jung to the coniunctio, and the latter to the symbol for Christ which is the fish. Jung saw this dream as signalling the fact that the 'cure of souls' rested with his parents which meant that it was still latent in Jung's own unconscious.

The dream also reminded Jung of the Grail legend and the suffering of the 'fisher king' Amfortas from the wound that would not heal. Jung says that this is the Christian suffering which he witnessed in his father and for which the alchemists sought the 'panacea'. The theriomorphic attributes of the gods denote that they dwell not only in the superhuman regions but also in the subhuman realms: 'as above so below' is an alchemical saying often quoted by Jung. It is this subversive, earthy imagery of alchemy, often expressed in animal form, that was compensatory to the sexlessness of medieval Christianity. As Jung says in the following quote: 'A person whose roots are above as well as below is thus like a tree growing simultaneously downwards and upwards. The goal is neither height nor depth, but the centre' (Jung, 1967: 264).

Kabbala

Allusions to the Kabbala, the Jewish mystical tradition, are scattered throughout the *Collected Works*, particularly in relation to the feminine principle or the male/female dichotomy. For Jung, as for the Kabbalists, the feminine 'is as often as not conventionally associated with darkness, negativity, even what we call evil' (Gottlieb, 1994: 63). She goes on to say that what Jung seems to have taken from the Kabbala is the concept that there is something disturbing about the feminine in a logical universe but that without the feminine there would be no life at all. This paradox led to the view of the feminine as a necessary evil.

In the *Bahir*, the first manuscript of the Jewish mystical tradition, the feminine tree is added after the nine masculine trees so that God's garden would endure. Jung transposes this notion on to the concept of the Trinity in Christianity. Originally the Trinity was all spiritual and therefore all masculine but room had to be found for the feminine. The fourth, the feminine, was added and with it the possibility of evil. Jung equated this feminine with the Shulamit of the Song of Songs who is 'black but beautiful' and 'comes from the same category as the black goddesses (Isis, Artemis, Parvati, Mary) whose names mean "earth"' (Jung, 1963a: 420).

Jung also resorts to the Kabbala when writing about the fragmentation and reintegration of the psyche. His 'description of the many sparks of a primal World Soul or collective unconscious is based on Kabbalistic and Hassidic notions of the "breaking of the vessels"' (Gottlieb, 1994: 67). It is in the unconscious that these sparks or scintillae are hidden and are like seeds of consciousness buried in the darkness.

A Kabbalist idea of the collaboration between Man and God was to have a huge impact on Jung and culminated in the writing of *Answer to Job*. This is found in the writings of Isaac Luria, a sixteenth-century Kabbalist, who says that in the act of creation, God formed vessels to contain the light but as they were too weak they broke. In this way, evil entered the world and since then everything was touched by the consequences of the split. It was Man who was called upon because of his consciousness to help God to overcome the split.

> The Jew has the advantage of having long since anticipated the develop-
> ment of consciousness in his own spiritual history. By this I mean the
> Lurianic stage of the Kabbalah, the breaking of the vessels and man's help
> in restoring them. Here the thought emerges for the first time that man
> must help God to repair the damage wrought by the Creation. For the first
> time man's cosmic responsibility is acknowledged. (Jaffé, 1989: 102).

Father Victor White

Victor White was an English Dominican priest and a reader in Theology at Blackfriars, Oxford. He was a founding member of the Jung Institute in Zurich and lectured widely on Jungian psychology seeking to reconcile it with religion. As a result of this relationship, Jung felt that he had at last encountered a member of the clergy who understood what he was trying to say. He bemoaned the fact that other theologians saw him as an atheistic metaphysician rather than as an agnostic psychologist. Only White 'has successfully undertaken to feel his way into the empiricist's manner of thinking as far as possible' (White, 1961: 307).

The issue that finally came between them was that of the doctrine of *privatio boni* or the Christian view of evil as the privation of good. For Jung, on the contrary, evil was a force in its own right and he insisted that Christianity had to include the devil in its concept of God. White parted company with him on this issue as he felt that in so doing, Jung was breaking his own self-imposed boundary of remaining within psychology and was now trespassing into the realm of theology. By doing so and by saying what he had about evil, what Jung was advocating was tantamount to heresy according to White.

> That is how the Christian doctrine gets out of its inherent dualism, i.e.,
> Manicheism, by denying the existence of Evil. You do deny it by calling
> Evil a decreasing Good. Absolute Evil is for you a merely neutral
> condition, in which there is nothing at all. (Adler, 1976: 73)

The main thrust of Jung's argument with Christianity is that it embodies a one-sided version of God and, by doing so, robs it of its essential diversity. Paradoxically, Jung also points to the *One* and it is this paradox that encapsulates the quintessence of Jung's religious viewpoint.

White felt let down when *Answer to Job* appeared as he had no idea that Jung actually intended publishing it. (Personal communication by Murray Stein, 1999). However, they never broke with each other completely and continued to correspond until White's death from cancer in 1960.

Answer to Job

Answer to Job, was a highly personal and emotional outpouring by Jung in which he tried to formulate ideas that had perplexed him throughout his life about the fundamental nature of evil and the 'tragic contradictoriness' of God.

The origins of the book lie in Jung's earlier one *Aion* where he had dealt with the psychology of Christianity. To quote Jung about why he felt impelled to write *Answer to Job*: 'The most immediate cause of my writing the book is perhaps to be found in certain problems discussed in my book *Aion*, especially the problems of Christ as a symbolic figure and of the antagonism Christ-Antichrist, represented in the traditional zodiacal symbolism of the two fishes' (Jung, 1958: ix).

In *Aion* there are references to the bright and dark side of divinity and this ambivalent God-image plays a crucial part in the *Book of Job*. For Jung, Job is a prefiguration of Christ – the link between them being the idea of suffering. As Jung says: 'In the final analysis it is God who created the world and its sins, and who therefore became Christ in order to suffer the fate of humanity' (Jung, 1963b: 243).

The problem of Job had manifested itself in a dream as so often happened at momentous times for Jung. This is another long dream in which he is accompanied by his father throughout and the following is the last part of it:

> We then entered the house, and I saw that it had very thick walls. We climbed a narrow staircase to the second floor. There a strange sight presented itself: a large hall which was the exact replica of the *divan-i-kaas* (council hall) of Sultan Akbar at Fatehpur Sikri. It was a high circular room with a gallery running along the wall, from which four bridges led to a basin-shaped centre. The basin rested upon a huge column and formed the sultan's round seat. From this elevated place he spoke to his councillors and philosophers, who sat along the walls in the gallery. The whole was a gigantic mandala. It corresponded precisely to the real *divan-i-kaas*.
>
> In the dream I suddenly saw that from the centre a steep flight of stairs ascended to a spot high up on the wall – which no longer corresponded

to reality. At the top of the stairs was a small door, and my father said, 'Now I will lead you into the highest presence.' Then he knelt down and touched his forehead to the floor. I imitated him, likewise kneeling, with great emotion. For some reason I could not bring my forehead quite down to the floor – there was perhaps a millimetre to spare. But at least I had made the gesture with him. Suddenly I knew – perhaps my father had told me – that that upper door led to a solitary chamber where lived Uriah, King David's general, whom David had shamefully betrayed for the sake of his wife Bathsheba, by commanding his soldiers to abandon Uriah in the face of the enemy. (Jung, 1963b: 246)

The Indian setting of the dream harks back to when Jung actually visited the sub-continent and was impressed by the mandala structure of the *divan-i-kaas* at the centre of which was the seat of Akbar the Great, who, like King David, is a worldly lord. But in the dream Uriah is placed highest as the guiltless victim who was abandoned by David. Jung sees Uriah as a pre-figuration of Christ who was abandoned by God. Furthermore, David had possessed himself of Uriah's wife. Jung only understood later the two reasons why Uriah featured in this dream when he felt himself impelled to speak out publicly about the ambivalence of the Old Testament God and Emma Jung was taken from him by death.

The lack of complete submission on his part in the dream signified for Jung that something in him was defiant just as it was in other free human beings as, for instance, those who wrote the *Book of Job*.

The main thrust of what Jung ends up saying about the *Book of Job* is that Job proves morally superior to God by withstanding all the trials that are heaped on him without losing faith. This so impresses divinity that the latter incarnates as Christ.

> Besides his love of mankind a certain irascibility is noticeable in Christ's character, and, as is often the case with people of emotional temperament, a manifest lack of self-reflection. There is no evidence that Christ ever wondered about himself, or that he ever confronted himself. To this rule there is only one significant exception – the despairing cry from the Cross: 'My God, my God, why hast thou forsaken me?' Here his human nature attains divinity; at that moment God experiences what it means to be a mortal man and drinks to the dregs what he made his faithful servant Job suffer. Here is given the answer to Job, and, clearly, this supreme moment is as divine as it is human, as 'eschatological' as it is 'psychological'. (Jung, 1958: 46)

He ends the book by saying: 'Strictly speaking, the God-image does not coincide with the unconscious as such, but with a special content of it, namely the archetype of the self. It is the archetype from which we can no longer distinguish the God-image empirically' (Jung, 1958: 107).

Jung's Writings

Reference will be made in the following pages to lengthy passages from two of Jung's works in order to give a fuller picture of how he elaborated ideas that he developed from the formative encounters he had with the thinkers discussed earlier in this chapter. His own theoretical formulations evolved over many years and he would add to or take out from published works as he went along. In this way, when revising any of his writings, he would do a cut-and-paste job and incorporate large amounts of new thinking in previously published texts.

The two works that will be referred to below have been selected because they provide good illustrations of his major theories. The first one is the *Psychology of the Unconscious: A Study of the Transformations and Symbolisms of the Libido*, which he was writing while still working closely with Freud. The second is *Psychological Types*, which was partly inspired by Jung's attempt to make sense of the subsequent break.

Psychology of the Unconscious: A Study of the
Transformations and Symbolisms of the Libido
This book was first published under the above title in 1912 and republished 37 years later under the title *Symbols of Transformation: An Analysis of the Prelude to a Case of Schizophrenia*. At the latter time, Jung revised it considerably, stating that it had been in urgent need of revision as when he wrote it he was under considerable pressure of work so that it consisted of 'larger or smaller fragments which I could only string together in an unsatisfying manner' (Jung, 1956: xxiii). His aim in writing it in the first place was as follows:

> One of my principal aims was to free medical psychology from the subjective and personalistic bias that characterized its outlook at that time, and to make it possible to understand the unconscious as an objective and collective psyche. The personalism in the views of Freud and Adler that went hand in hand with the individualism of the nineteenth century failed to satisfy me because, except in the case of instinctive dynamisms (which actually have too little place in Adler), it left no room for objective, impersonal facts. Freud, accordingly, could see no objective justification for my attempt, but suspected personal motives. (Jung, 1956: xxiv)

Looking back from the perspective of 37 years, Jung declared in the Foreword to the new edition that the need to write the book in the first place arose out of his growing interest in mythology and in discovering his own myth. The book laid down the programme he was to follow for the next few decades of his life which was his growing concern with the mythological and symbolical realm that underlay consciousness. As he expresses it:

> Individual consciousness is only the flower and the fruit of a season, sprung from the perennial rhizome beneath the earth; and it would find itself in better accord with the truth if it took the existence of the rhizome into its calculations. For the root matter is the mother of all things. (Jung, 1956: xxiv)

The book was written in his 36th year, which marks for Jung the second half of life when a mental transformation often takes place in individuals. It was to mark the beginning of his life's work where the real patient in the book is Jung himself embarking on his own individuation process. As mentioned above, this entailed a five-year-long confrontation with the unconscious and I have written elsewhere of the nexus between major rites of passage and the constellation of archetypal shadow.

The references to this work will concentrate on the original 1912 version reissued in 1991 with an introduction by William McGuire, in which he points out the huge amount of extraverted activity that Jung was caught up in between the years 1909–11. His personal life at this time was demanding – he had a wife and four children and was building a home at Küsnacht to house them all. He gave up his position at the Burghölzli and launched his private practice; was the President of the International Psychoanalytic Association and Editor of the Yearbook; wrote eight articles and two dozen notices; travelled to the USA and to various parts of Europe; fulfilled his Swiss military service for one month of each year; was involved in training younger analysts, including J.J. Honegger and Sabina Spielrein. Both contributed to the *Psychology of the Unconscious*, which he was writing at the same time as his involvement in the above activities.

As McGuire goes on to say, the progress of the book is reflected in the correspondence with Freud and the first letter containing hints of his growing interest in mythology and symbolism is in October 1909, immediately after the trip to America with Freud and Ferenzi. Mention of the book occurs from then on in the correspondence between the two and Freud responds positively to the growing references to mythology on Jung's part.

Around 1910 Frank Miller is first mentioned in the Freud/Jung correspondence edited by McGuire in 1974. It is her automatic writing at the request of her psychiatrist Théodore Flournoy that is to set Jung off on his creative writing that has its end result in the book. Jung is now warning Freud in a letter dated 13 December, to be prepared to read something from him 'the like of which you have never heard from me'. However, he continues to keep the manuscript from Freud who writes on 22 January 1911: 'I don't know why you are so afraid of my criticism in matters of mythology.' In fact, Freud is himself working on a mythological piece that eventually became *Totem and Taboo*.

In March 1911 came the suicide of Honegger, which was mourned by both Jung and Freud. The former's work was of enormous importance in Jung's discovery of the collective unconscious, with the following piece of work he had done with a patient:

> Honegger discovered the following hallucination in an insane man (paranoid dement): The patient sees in the sun an 'upright tail' similar to an erected penis. When he moves his head back and forth, then, too, the sun's penis sways back and forth in a like manner, and out of that the wind arises. This strange hallucination remained unintelligible to us for a long time until I became acquainted with the Mithraic liturgy and its visions. (Jung, 1991: 96)

The Mithraic liturgy cited by Jung coincided closely with the vision of the patient and the importance of this coincidence can be seen from the following written statement by Freud:

> For everyone involved in the development of psychoanalysis when C.G. Jung, at a private scientific gathering, reported through one of his students that the fantasies of certain mental patients (dementia praecox) coincided strikingly with the mythological cosmogonies of ancient peoples of whom these uneducated patients could not possibly have had any scholarly knowledge. (Jung, 1991: xxiii)

Shortly before the Third Psychoanalytical Congress in Weimar, Freud spent four days with Jung and his wife in September 1911 at Küsnacht. This appears to have been a tense visit as a few weeks after this Emma Jung wrote to Freud: 'Since your visit I have been tormented by the idea that your relation with my husband is not altogether as it should be . . .' (Jung, 1991: xxi). She goes on to say that she suspects that Freud is not agreeable to the book as he did not speak of it at all even though Jung was awaiting his verdict with great trepidation.

Although there was no visible sign of tension at the Weimar Congress, and the tenor of their correspondence appears amiable on the surface, yet McGuire writes:

> What could be called a collision course now becomes evident in the exchange. Both men swing between extremes of affect. There are fewer instances of the wit and grace, the friendliness, that had often brightened the letters. Freud appears patient, yet clearly uneasy over Jung's direction. (Jung, 1991: xxiii)

Following this came the unfortunate 'Kreuzlingen gesture' when Freud travelled to Kreuzlingen, situated on the Swiss side of Lake Constance, to visit the sick Ludwig Binswanger. He did not go on to visit Jung who, not knowing of Binswanger's illness, took it as a personal insult. A full account of the Freud/Jung rupture is given elsewhere in this book.

The *Psychology of the Unconscious* was translated into English by Beatrice Hinkle, an American physician who became the city physician of San Francisco, the first American woman to hold such a post. It was her work with victims of the bubonic plague and their varying reactions to it that led to her taking up the practice of psychotherapy. She moved to the east coast and established the first psychotherapy clinic in the USA at the medical school of Cornell University. She came to Europe to have analysis with Freud or one of his disciples but was immediately drawn to Jung's approach and after the break between him and Freud, she chose to remain in the Jungian camp.

When the *Psychology of the Unconscious* was first published in English in 1916 by an American publisher Hinkle wrote an introduction to it that included the following:

> It is this great theme (the self-sacrifice motive) which Jung sees as the real motive lying hidden in the myths and religions of man from the beginning, as well as in the literature and artistic creations of both ancient and modern time, and which he works out with the greatest wealth of detail and painstaking effort in the book herewith presented. (Jung, 1991: xxix)

Hinkle also persuaded Jung to let her divide the long Chapter VI, 'The Battle of Deliverance from the Mother', into a second chapter entitled, 'The Dual Mother', Chapter VII. In 1925, Jung brought out an unrevised second edition of the book in which he stated that the late Théodore Flournoy had told him that he – Jung – 'had hit off her mentality very well. Valuable confirmation of this reached me in 1918, through an American colleague who was treating Frank Miller for the schizophrenic disturbance which had broken out after her sojourn in Europe' (Jung, 1991: xxx).

Sonu Shamdasani's (1990) paper, *A Woman Called Frank*, describes Frank Miller as 'Jung's Imago' – 'imago' being the term used at the time of writing the *Psychology of the Unconscious* before he changed it to 'archetype'. In 1912, Jung was predisposed to diagnose her as a case of schizophrenia as a result of his linking mythology to that disorder as we have seen above. When he later revised the text, the emphasis had changed for him to the attitude of consciousness to mythological phenomena and he pathologizes

Frank Miller as having 'not the faintest idea of what is happening. . .' (Jung, 1956: 397).

> It is hardly to be supposed that Miss Miller, who evidently had not the faintest clue as to the real meaning of her visions – which even Théodore Flournoy, despite his fine feeling for values, could do nothing to explain – would be able to meet the next phase of the process, namely the assimilation of the hero to her conscious personality, with the right attitude . . . The instinctual impulse that was trying to rouse the dreamer from the sleep of childhood was opposed by a personal pride that was distinctly out of place, and also, one must suppose by a correspondingly narrow moral horizon. (Jung, 1956: 441)

We see Jung here applying his theory of teleology rather too astringently and giving the patient a good telling off for failing to come up to scratch. Even the previously much-admired Flournoy comes in for a bit of a dressing down. It is salutory to read the earlier and later editions side-by-side as an example of the radical revisions that Jung would make to previous texts.

Libido   Throughout the three chapters on libido in the *Psychology of the Unconscious*, one can see Jung working out his own theory of libido and using his method of amplification to elaborate it. As is apparent by now from what has already been said above, Jung never wholeheartedly accepted Freud's version and in the *Psychology of the Unconscious* he is now embarking on his own concept of psychic energy. Jung acknowledges that Freud had also come to realize the need to widen the concept of libido after his famous examination of the Schreber case, where the longed for reality may be traced back not only to the withdrawal of the libidinous impulses.

In exploring his own theorizing in this direction, Jung returns both to his work with schizophrenic patients and to Janet's *'fonction du réel'* or the reality function. With regard to the former, Jung says that he was unable to establish the theory of this psychosis based on the concept of the displacement of libido. The whole of the function of reality is lacking to such a degree that movement of any kind is lost to the patient, as in catatonic schizophrenia.

He could, however, see the validity of Freud's libido theory when applied to the transference neuroses where the erotic libido has been repressed followed by regression into an earlier path of transference, for instance, that of the parental transference. Yet here again, Jung claims that it is only that portion of the libido which is tied up in the neurosis which is lacking to the patient. The rest of the libido related to adaptation to reality is still available.

Following on from this, Jung then takes issue with Abraham's theory that the withdrawal of sexual libido from the outer world results in paranoid or schizophrenic symptomatology. Again the transference of sexual libido to schizophrenia is impossible because this illness produces a loss of reality that cannot be put at the door of deficiency of libido defined in the narrow sense.

Jung then puts forward the hypothesis that in the history of evolution there was a gradual diminution in the animal kingdom of the general impulse to propagate. This has led to the displacement of the procreative instinct onto mechanisms of allurement limited to the breeding season and to protection of the young. Even if there can be no doubt that everything has its origins in sexual libido 'it would be a poor, unaesthetic generalization if one were to include music in the category of sexuality. A similar nomenclature would then lead us to classify the cathedral of Cologne as mineralogy because it is built of stones' (Jung, 1991: 130).

The transformation of primal libido into non-sexualized functions is still taking place and where the individual succeeds in adapting to it it is called 'sublimation'. Where it is pathological it is termed 'repression'. So, for Jung, when an individual takes his libido away from investment in the outer world, the energy is taken away from those desexualized instincts which properly support the function of reality.

Jung here returns to the confrontation with Abraham's theory of sexualized libido in hysteria and schizophrenia. Jung agrees that hysterical introversion of the sexualized libido leads to autoerotism because the person's erotic influx of libido, which is designed for reality functioning, becomes transferred to the ego.

The schizophrenic shuns reality to a much greater degree than the influx of sexualized libido would account for so that his inner condition is radically different from the hysteric's. The inner condition here is more than autoerotic and there is, instead, an intra-psychic equivalent of reality which is invested with dynamics other than sexualized libido. For this reason, Jung agrees with Bleuler's rejection of the concept of autoerotism taken by Abraham from the study of hysteria and applied to schizophrenia. When dealing with the latter, Bleuler proposed replacing autoerotism with autism.

Having offered his revised genetic theory of libido in relation to schizophrenia, Jung goes on to explore whether this revised theory would also apply to the neuroses. He decides that it does because temporary functional disturbances appear in the neuroses which go beyond the boundaries of the sexual, for instance, in psychotic episodes.

Jung then begins a fascinating exploration of the 'as if' which arises out of his proposition that the replacement of the disturbed function of reality is affected by an archaic or mythological surrogate. He quotes Spielrein in support of this as follows: 'I often had the illusion that these patients might be simply victims of a folk superstition' (Jung, 1991: 137). The vision of the alchemist, Zosimos, often cited by Jung, showed that superstitions were once symbols and it is these that provide the bridges for partial amounts of libido to pass over into the mental realm. For instance, where the union of two transference symbols to replace the generative organs may be used culturally to explain the origin of humankind. As Jung says: 'The propelling motive of this transition of the *immediate sexual* libido to the non-sexual representation can, in my opinion, be found only in a *resistance which opposes primitive sexuality*' (Jung, 1991: 138).

This fantasy analogy formation would lead to increasing amounts of libido becoming desexualized as new objects became assimilated as sexual symbols. Jung even conjectures that human consciousness may have been arrived at entirely in this way. As we saw above, Jung is using Miller's writing as the raw material from which there might come a possible transformation of the libido into the heroic quest for consciousness. It is also the source of human discoveries which he then sets out to demonstrate by amplifying case material from one of his patients.

The patient was suffering from a depressive catatonic condition that Jung was treating analytically, in the course of which, she fell into a hysterical, dream-like state displaying evidence of sexual excitement. She started to masturbate and, at the same time, made a '*violent rotary motion*' (Jung's italics) with the forefinger of the left hand on her left temple, as if she were boring a hole there.

Boring into bodily orifices, nail-biting, finger-sucking, and picking at parts of the body are linked to infantile sexual activity which may often persist into adulthood. Jung consulted with the patient's mother who confirmed that as a child, the patient would rhythmically beat her head against the door. Later, she began to bore a hole with her finger in the wall plaster keeping herself occupied with this activity for hours at a time. From the age of four she began to masturbate.

In order to bring the major themes – libido, sun/fire, boring – that he has been exploring in these chapters into some sort of relationship with each other, Jung now embarks on a process of amplification which links mythical thinking across different cultures. This will be elaborated further in the next chapter.

Abraham's book on *Dreams and Myths*, took up some of the discoveries of Adalbert Kuhn in his work *Mythologische Studien*.

Kuhn links the Greek Prometheus, who was the fire-bringer, with the Hindu Pramantha, the masculine fire-rubbing piece of wood. 'The path from Pramantha to Prometheus passes not through the word, but through the idea, and, therefore, we should adopt this same meaning for Prometheus as that which Pramantha attains from the Hindu fire symbolism' (Jung, 1991: 144).

In this way, Jung came to broaden the psychoanalytic concept of libido with his own metaphor of psychic energy. Basically, Jung's approach to psychic energy is concerned with meaning and with the symbols of transformation that accompany changes in the direction of the flow of energy.

Psychological Types

> Plato and Aristotle! These are not merely two systems, they are types of two distinct human natures, which from time immemorial, under every sort of disguise, stand more or less inimically opposed . . . Although under other names, it is always of Plato and Aristotle that we speak. Visionary, mystical, Platonic natures disclose Christian ideas and the corresponding symbols from the fathomless depths of their souls. Practical, orderly, Aristotelian natures build out of these ideas and symbols a fixed system, a dogma and a cult. Finally the Church embraces both natures, one of them entrenched in the clergy and the other in monasticism, but both keeping up a constant feud. (Jung, 1971: 2)

The above quote from Heine is at the front of the book Jung wrote during his fallow period from 1913–17 in which he was trying to differentiate himself from Freud and Adler and to understand the rift that had recently taken place between the three of them. As an empiricist – something that Jung emphasized about himself over and over again – he also had a broader interest in trying to understand the conflicts and misunderstandings that arise in human interactions in every situation.

Psychological Types is an early work in which we see Jung's ideas taking shape, for instance, his incipient thinking on archetypes. His Kantian bias is evident in the book as he takes up the discussion that he comes back to many times in his writings. This is centred on whether or not the mind is originally *tabula rasa*, that is a blank slate in which ideas are only epiphenomenal abstractions from outer experience. Kant demonstrated that certain categories of thinking are *a priori*, that is innate and prior to all experience. Jung takes these Kantian ideas and applies them to his own thinking about the brain as the depository of patterns of phylogenetic experiences and attempts at adaptation.

These patterns of experience are by no means accidental or arbitrary; they follow strictly preformed conditions which are not transmitted by experience as contents of apprehension but are the preconditions of all apprehension . . . We may think of them, as Plato did, as *images*, as schemata, or as inherited functional possibilities. (Jung, 1971: 304)

Jung proposes two mechanisms – introversion and extraversion – both of which are at work in all humans. It is only the relative predominance of the one over the other that determines whether an individual is more extraverted or introverted. The extraverted attitude depicts a movement of interest outwards to the object; the introverted attitude, on the other hand, results in a movement of interest inwards to the subject.

Having identified two groups of psychological individuals, Jung then goes on to say that within each there are huge differences between individuals making up the group. Jung came to see empirically that there were also psychological functions that differentiate individuals from one another and identified these as *thinking, feeling, sensation* and *intuition*. Furthermore, each of these functions is either predominantly *extraverted* or *introverted*. In this way, Jung ends up identifying eight possible types that go to make up his scheme of psychological types.

William James

William James was, in part, the inspiration for *Psychological Types*, with his division of temperament into two kinds which he identified as the 'rationalist' and the 'empiricist'. The former is 'your devotee of abstract and eternal principles'; the latter the 'lover of facts in all their crude variety' (Jung, 1971: 300). James goes on to make 'rationalism' equate with 'intellectualism' and 'empiricism' with 'sensationalism'. James summarizes both types with his well-known dichotomy of 'tender-minded' for the 'rationalist' and 'tough-minded' for the 'empiricist'.

They have a low opinion of each other. Their antagonism, whenever as individuals their temperaments have been intense, has formed in all pages a part of the philosophic atmosphere of the time. It forms a part of the atmosphere today. The tough think of the tender as sentimentalists and soft-heads. The tender feel the tough to be unrefined, callous, or brutal . . . Each type believes the other to be inferior to itself. (Jung, 1971: 301)

The qualities that James associates with the 'tender-minded' type are: rationalistic; intellectualistic; idealistic; optimistic; religious; free-willist; monistic; dogmatical. Those he associates with the 'tough-minded' are: empiricist; sensationalistic; materialistic; pessimistic; irreligious; fatalistic; pluralistic; sceptical. The 'rationalistic' is broken down further into 'going by principles' and the 'empiricist' into 'going by facts'. The 'sensationalistic' in James's model denotes extreme empiricism where sensory experience is the exclusive source of knowing.

Jung acknowledged James's contribution in drawing attention to the importance of temperament in relation to philosophical thinking. His criticism of this approach is two-fold: one that it is biased towards pragmatism, the American philosophical movement derived from English philosophy which regards practical efficacy and usefulness to be the highest 'truth'. James was, of course, an adherent of pragmatism. The other criticism is that although James brings the psychological equation into his model, it is concerned only with 'thinking'. This was, of course, James's area of interest but nevertheless restricts his model to the study of intellectual capacities coloured by temperament.

The Apollinian and the Dionysian

The Birth of Tragedy was written by Nietzsche in 1871 while he was still enamoured of Schopenhauer whose idea of 'wills' Nietzsche was later to reject and replace with his own of the 'will to power'. Schopenhauer was captivated by the East, which Nietzsche adapted to his own purposes in seeing Greece as the meeting point between East and West.

In this early work, the portrait of Greece that Nietzsche presents is full of darkness and dread and his contention is that the Greeks had to create the Olympian gods out of the sheer terror and frightfulness of existence which he encapsulates thus:

> Moira pitilessly enthroned above all knowledge, the vulture of Pro-
> metheus the great friend of man, the awful fate of the wise Oedipus, the
> family curse of the Atrides that drove Orestes to matricide . . . all this
> dread was ever being conquered anew by the Greeks with the help of that
> visionary, intermediate world of the Olympians. (Jung, 1971: 137)

In this book, Nietzsche has set out to describe his oppositional pair, which he calls the *Apollinian* and the *Dionysian*. He describes them as follows: 'the continuous development of art is bound up with the duality of the Apollinian and the Dionysian, in much the same way as generation depends on the duality of the sexes, involving per-petual conflicts with only periodic reconciliations' (Jung, 1971: 137). These two deities were the gods of the arts and in their very opposition they provoke each other to higher achievements – one as the shaper, the other as the Dionysian art of music. 'Finally, by a metaphysical miracle of the Hellenic "will", they appear paired one with the other, and from this mating the equally Apollinian and

Dionysian creation of Attic tragedy is at last brought to birth' (Jung, 1971: 138).

The psychological states that they give rise to are depicted by Nietzsche as *dreaming* and *intoxication*. The former, he characterizes as belonging to the Apollinian impulse which produces an 'inward vision' and a 'lovely semblance of dream-worlds'. Apollo signifies limitation and the subjugation of the wild and untamed things in life.

The Dionysian impulse, on the other hand, means the breaking loose of animal and divine nature resulting in the liberation of instinct. Its manifestation is the satyr, half-man, half-goat that signified the dissolution of humans into their collective instincts. 'All the artistry of Nature is revealed in the ecstasies of intoxication' and 'man is no longer the artist, he has become the work of art' writes Nietzsche of the Dionysian state (Jung, 1971: 139). The well-known Dionysian orgies are described by him as follows:

> Practically everywhere the central point of these festivals lay in exuberant sexual licence, which swamped all family life and its venerable traditions; the most savage bestialities of nature were unleashed, including that atrocious amalgam of lust and cruelty which has always seemed to me the true witch's broth. (Jung, 1971: 139)

Nietzsche's proposition is that it was the reconciliation of the oppositional forces of Apollo and Dionysus that resulted in the Greek civilization where the antagonism between them is 'seemingly bridged by the common term "Art"' (Jung, 1971: 139). Jung points to this as the central problem in Nietzsche's thinking which remains stuck in aesthetics. For Jung, the reconciliation between these two forces was not an aesthetic but a religious one and Greek tragedy arose out of a religious ceremony: the cult of Dionysus.

> Aestheticism can, of course, take the place of the religious function. But how many things are there that could not do the same? What have we not come across at one time or another as a substitute for the absence of religion? Even though aestheticism may be a very noble substitute, it is nevertheless only a compensation for the real thing that is lacking. Moreover, Nietzsche's later 'conversion' to Dionysus best shows that the aesthetic substitute did not stand the test of time. (Jung, 1971: 141)

Nietzsche equated the Dionysian with saying 'yes' to life and attacked Socrates in *The Birth of Tragedy* for his over-reliance on rationalism which upset the balance that had been struck by the ancient Greeks by 'a metaphysical miracle of the Hellenic "will"' (Jung, 1971: 143). As he was still profoundly under the influence of Schopenhauer at the time of writing, the metaphysical will means the unconscious.

The importance of Nietzsche's Apollonian/Dionysian opposition for Jung lay in leading him to elaborate his own typological scheme. The Apollinian attitude leads to the production of ideas – in a thinking person it leads to intellectual ideas; in a feeling person it results in feeling-toned ideas. The latter would relate to the idea of freedom, immorality and the fatherland. These two – thinking and feeling – are essentialy rational and logical.

However, Jung saw that Nietzsche's model had evolved in a particular way because of the latter's aesthetic approach to life and from here Jung went on to develop the principles of a third and fourth function – sensation and intuition. These are the non-rational modes of functioning and Jung relates these to Nietzsche's typology. He was an extreme introvert and an intuitive – Jung deduces this from his lack of rational moderation. His sensation lay repressed in him and he experienced it largely through his intuition which gave him deep insights into the Dionysian qualities in his unconscious.

Prometheus and Epimetheus

Nietzsche's dyad owes a great deal to the opposition between the Promethean, forward-looking attitude and the Epimethean, back-ward-looking one portrayed in Goethe's *Faust*. Goethe's drama is the medieval version of the one he took from antiquity and adapted to his own time so that it is a medieval Prometheus in the form of Faust, and a medieval Epimetheus in the form of Mephistopheles that confront each other even though it becomes evident that they are the same person. Once again it is the divine wager between good and evil that is being played out.

The passion that the Greek Epimetheus had for Pandora becomes the diabolical plot of Mephistopheles for the soul of Faust. The Greek Prometheus's cunning in turning down Pandora becomes in Faust the tragedy of Gretchen and the belated fulfilment of the yearning for Helen. This is the medieval transformation of the wor-ship of God into the worship of woman which denotes the worship of the soul – herein lie the beginnings of modern individualism.

> Faust's redemption began at his death. The divine, Promethean character he had preserved all his life fell away from him only at death, with his rebirth. Psychologically, this means that the Faustian attitude must be abandoned before the individual can become an integrated whole. The figure that first appeared as Gretchen and then on a higher level as Helen, and was finally exalted as the Mater Gloriosa, is a symbol whose many meanings cannot be discussed here. Suffice to say that it is the same primordial image that lies at the heart of Gnosticism, the image of the divine harlot – Eve, Helen, Mary, Sophia. (Jung, 1971: 188)

The Promethean defiance of the accepted gods is personified in *Faust* in the form of the medieval magician: a figure that is pre-Christian and imbued with the pagan unconscious. He is a destroyer but also a saviour who is pre-eminently suited to resolve the conflict of opposites depicted in the drama. In Jungian terms this figure came to be called the *Trickster*, the symbolic bearer of an attempt to resolve the conflict of opposites between Prometheus/Epimetheus; Apollo/Dionysus; Faust/Mephistopheles; conscious/unconscious; introversion/extraversion.

General Description of the Types

Jung finishes his book with a definition of the two attitudes – extraversion and introversion – and of the four types – thinking, feeling, intuition, sensation. As each of the latter is either extraverted or introverted, this results in eight possible types, i.e. *extraverted thinking*; *introverted thinking*; *extraverted feeling*; *introverted feeling*; *extraverted intuition*; *introverted intuition*; *extraverted sensation*; *introverted sensation*. In each instance, an extreme example of the type is on offer in order to give as clear a picture as possible of what is being described. It would be as well to bear this in mind as in reality there are few living examples of pristine types of any of the below.

The Extraverted Type: The Conscious Attitude

Jung makes a distinction between the conscious and unconscious attitude in both the extraverted and the introverted types. To take first the conscious attitude, Jung has this to say: 'If a man thinks, feels, acts, and actually lives in a way that is *directly* correlated with the objective conditions and their demands, he is extraverted' (Jung, 1971: 333). In this way, orientation by the object predominates. For instance, the fact that everybody follows a certain mode of fashion at any one time while one person chooses the opposite means that that person is an extravert because their choice is dictated by the outer objective event and not the subjective view. Jung likens the extraverted attitude to Epimetheus who adjusts to the moral standpoint governing society at any one time because for the extravert no other criterion exists. However, as Jung goes on to point out, that does not mean that the extraverted individual is well-adapted as the moral standpoint of a society may in fact at any one point be abnormal. In this way, the capacity for adjustment of the extravert is their limitation as true adaptation means more than a temporary fitting-in with the demands of the moment.

The danger for the extravert is of being 'sucked into the object' with a resultant loss of the self. An extraverted businessperson may be completely taken over by the demands of an expanding business and both the individual's psychological and physiological needs suffer. This is because even the body is not sufficiently 'out there' to be seen as 'objective'. The end result is usually a compensatory illness or symptoms forcing a change upon the individual.

The pathological side of extreme extraversion may result in some of the following symptoms. A performer whose fame has reached meteoric heights may experience stage fright and an ambitious person who has over-extended themselves may have bouts of mountain sickness. Jung says that hysteria is the most frequent neurosis associated with this type. This displays itself in some of the following ways: a need to impress others, effusiveness, or a morbid intensification of fantasy life as the libido is forced to introvert to the unconscious.

The Unconscious Attitude   The unconscious attitude of the extravert will be compensatory to the individual's total immersion in the object and thus be of a corresponding primitive, infantile and egocentric nature. This is a result of the repression of all the inner impulses of thoughts, wishes, affects and needs which leaves them deprived of psychic energy. What is left over of the latter has a potency that Jung describes as 'primordial instinct' and the resultant 'egoism which characterizes the extravert's unconscious attitude goes far beyond mere childish selfishness; it verges on the ruthless and the brutal' (Jung, 1971: 339).

Whenever the unconscious emerges it does so in an exaggerated form and in complete opposition to the conscious attitude resulting in a catastrophic collision between the two. Jung exemplifies this with the case of a printer who worked his way up until he became the owner of a successful business of his own, eventually becoming completely gripped by it. The unconscious compensation of this exclusive immersion in his business was a regression to pleasurable childhood memories of enjoying painting and drawing. He then incorporated his infantile fantasies into the business which began to suffer and eventually went downhill.

Another pathological outcome is that there can develop a dangerous split between consciousness and the unconscious resulting in a nervous breakdown or to substance abuse and addiction. This is the result of the loss of the compensatory function which, instead, turns destructive and there is open conflict between the two realms.

Jung's model also proposes that one function will be superior – i.e. be under conscious control – while the other functions are more or less unconscious and display a haphazard or even primitive character. 'The superior function is always an expression of the conscious personality, of its aims, will, and general performance, whereas the less differentiated functions fall into the category of things that simply "happen" to one' (Jung, 1971: 340). The latter do not necessarily manifest only as slips of the tongue or oversights because there is a degree of consciousness attached to them. A telling example of this is the person with a superior extraverted feeling function who has an excellent rapport with everyone but sometimes expresses tactless opinions. The latter spring from an inferior, half-conscious thinking function.

Extraverted Thinking   Thinking has two sources: one that stems from subjective largely unconscious data and the other which is a response to objective data as experienced through sensory perception. The extraverted thinking type falls into the latter category and objective events or ideas will be the criteria on which judgment is passed. The direction of the thinking is also important in deciding whether someone is an extraverted thinking. The practical thinking of some scientists, technologists or business people that stem from objective data and have an outward application are examples of this type. So, too, is the philosopher who derives his ideas from tradition or the generally accepted thoughts of the time and the result will represent a higher level of collective facts.

Extraverted thinking is captivated by the object and can only reach its fulfilment when it is directed into a general idea. In this way, it can come to seem rather banal and if the objective data predominate over the act of thinking, the thinking may become sterile and manifest as a mere Epimethean 'after-thought'. A pathological outcome of this can be the assimilation of an oppressive amount of empirical material or the ruling object may become the principle by which life is governed. This can result in a form of tyranny over the person and over others within their domain.

In its extreme form, the compensatory feeling function may be repressed into the unconscious. This would include aesthetic activities, friendship and matters of taste. Non-rational phenomena likewise are repressed, including passion and religious experience – the latter sometimes emerging in a self-seeking form of altruism or ethical stance underlying which is a ruthless pursuit of their own ends using whatever means are necessary.

Extraverted Feeling   This kind of feeling detaches itself from any subjective qualities and is orientated only to objective data. Adjustment to the general feeling situation is all-important so a thing will be judged 'good' or 'beautiful' if it fits with the current view. All collective activity is motivated by this function, examples of this being church-going, fashion, attendance at the theatre and concerts. It has enormous creative potential in this way and, for instance, harmonious social life is generated by extraverted feeling on a large scale.

The extraverted feeling type will appear to be in harmony with external conditions and will, for instance, choose the 'right' spouse or partner in terms of age, social position, income, etc. On an individual level it has a salutary effect until the person becomes assimilated into the object, whereupon the individual quality of the feeling gets lost, leaving a cold 'unfeeling' person in its place. Another danger is the emergence of the repressed thinking function which can take the form of obsessive ideas, often of a negative kind.

Extraverted Sensation   Jung's term of sensation is applied to one of the perceiving functions and derives from sensory perception. In its extraverted form it is wholly dependent on the object and concrete processes to excite sensations and its orientation to 'reality' is unsurpassed. This latter may be mistaken for an acute rational function but, in fact, there exists no capacity for reflection and sensation types are at the mercy of their sensations, which are irrational. The vulgar extreme of this type will manifest in gross and sensual behaviour but there is also the aesthete who displays great purity of taste.

This type will be well-dressed, keep a good table and be drawn to the sybaritic life. The negative side of extraverted sensation manifests in crude forms of pleasure-seeking or an unscrupulous aesthetism. In the extreme form, the regressed intuitive function will manifest as a form of grotesque morality or superstitiousness.

Extraverted Intuition   Intuition is the function of unconscious perception and is 'represented in consciousness by an attitude of expectancy, by vision and penetration' (Jung, 1971: 366). Like sensation, when it is the dominant function it is not mere perception but an active process which puts into the object as much as it takes from it. The extraverted intuitive has a keen nose for anything that is in potential and is always seeking out new possibilities. Entrepreneurs are typically extraverted intuitives and they are known for their enormous energy in starting projects and then cold-bloodedly abandoning them when they begin to feel over-familiar and suffocating.

> His capacity to inspire courage or to kindle enthusiasm for anything new is unrivalled, although he may already have dropped it by the morrow . . . He brings his vision to life, he presents it convincingly and with dramatic fire, he embodies it, so to speak . . . it is a kind of fate. (Jung, 1971: 369)

The repressed sensation function in this type means that in the extreme form, the extraverted intuitive can never be grounded in the moment but lives always in a world of possibilities and may easily fritter away their life leaving others to reap the benefits of the fruits of their labour. Thinking and feeling may also function in an infantile, archaic way and give rise to suspicious fears and forebodings of illness.

The Introverted Type: The Conscious Attitude [Perception and cognition are not purely objective but subjective as well and introverts orientate their lives by subjective factors. It is not that introverted consciousness is unaware of external conditions but it responds to them in a subjectively determined way.] In this way, the introvert relies largely on the inner impression constellated by the object. Subjective reality is as real as objective and the introverted attitude is largely related to psychic adaptation.

The introvert derives its conscious attitude from the realm of the collective unconscious or, more specifically, the self. This is then represented in the form of preferences and definite ways of looking at things and usually equated by the individual with their ego. These subjective tendencies are taken to be identical with the object by the individual experiencing them but, in fact, have their origin in the unconscious and are merely released by the effect of the object.

These perceptions superimpose themselves on all outer objects:

> Thus, just as it seems incomprehensible to the introvert that the object should always be the decisive factor, it remains an enigma to the extravert how a subjective standpoint can be superior to the objective situation. He inevitably comes to the conclusion that the introvert is either a conceited egoist or crack-brained bigot. (Jung, 1971: 377)

Introverts can come across as inflexible in their subjective pronouncements and as their perceptions stem from the realm of the unconscious, find it difficult to validate their subjective judgements and perceptions. As a result of the merging of the ego with the self, the introvert's world-creating powers become concentrated in the ego and can lead to inflation and egocentricity.

The Unconscious Attitude   As the subjective factor predominates in the introvert's consciousness there is a corresponding devaluation of the object. The opposite state then is to be found here to the extravert's over-valuing of the object. As a result, the ego may become identified with the subject and increasingly defensive in its approach to objective data. However, it is not an easy matter to deny the power of the latter and the compensatory unconscious attitude of the introvert can become possessed by that power.

This results in a compulsive unconscious tie to objective data and the ego ends by being enslaved by them.

> The individual's freedom of mind is fettered by the ignominy of his financial dependence, his freedom of action trembles in the face of public opinion, his moral superiority collapses in a morass of inferior relationships, and his desire to dominate ends in a pitiful craving to be loved. (Jung, 1971: 378)

There ensues a conflict between the unconscious tie to the object and the conscious feelings of superiority towards the same. The ego becomes increasingly defensive in its relations with objects and the personal unconscious is gripped by powerful fantasies towards them. The end result is a terror of falling under the hostile influence of objects operating in him in an unconscious and archaic way and objects become endowed with magical powers.

The pathological state associated with introversion is psychasthenia, which is characterized by extreme sensitivity and chronic fatigue.

Introverted Thinking   As the following four types are, to all intents and purposes, the opposite of what has been written above about the introverted forms, they will be described more succinctly than those above.

This form of thinking is primarily orientated by the subjective factor and does not lead from outer experience back to objects. Instead, it begins and ends with the subject. Its intention is to create new views or theories about things rather than to establish new facts and in its extreme form leads to a kind of mystical thinking which is more to do with images than ideas. This can lead to a symbolic approach but if the ego becomes inflated then this access to the unconscious becomes blocked and the result is a 'veritable "pandaemonium" of irrational and magical figures' (Jung, 1971: 382).

Well-known illustrations of the two types of thinking – extraverted and introverted – are Darwin as an example of the former and Kant of the latter.

Introverted Feeling   The same things that have been said above about introverted thinking may equally be said about this type except that in this instance everything is felt rather than thought. Objects serve only as stimuli for the kind of imagery that is intensely sought after and all objects that do not fit with this are unheeded.

The positive aspect of this type is that it appears to the outer world as harmonious, sympathetic and usually in a state of pleasant repose – in summary it may said of it that 'still waters run deep'. The other side of this picture is that it is given to negative judgements or even a defensive appearance of profound indifference. The form of neurosis associated with this type in its pathological state is neurasthenia which manifests in feelings of exhaustion.

Introverted Sensation   Sensory perception is dependent on the object but in the introverted form it is the subjective aspect of the perception that is paramount. Jung places artists firmly in this category and says that if several painters were asked to paint the same landscape, each would be significantly different to the others because of the subjective way in which each would be interpreted.

Introverted sensation is governed by the intensity of subjective sensation excited by objective stimuli and in its positive aspect comes across as calm and self-controlled. The pathological side manifests itself in a compulsive disorder accompanied by symptoms of exhaustion.

Introverted Intuition   The orientation here is to inner objects which are synonymous with the contents of the unconscious. The subjective factor here is dominant and although the intuition may be stimulated by external objects, it is not concerned with them per se but with the impetus this has activated internally. Intuition looks around corners and perceives all the background processes of consciousness, however, in contrast to the extraverted version that continually seeks out possibilities in the environment, the introverted intuitive moves from image to image 'chasing after every possibility in the teeming womb of the unconscious' (Jung, 1971: 400). This is the realm of the archetypes, the a priori inherited foundations of the unconscious.

What intuition shares in common with sensation is that it is a perceiving rather than a judging function so that an aesthetic orientation predominates over a moral one as in thinking and feeling. The negative corollary of this function is that it is often out-of-step with the prevailing climate of opinion and is thought of as 'the voice of one crying in the wilderness'. The pathological neurosis here is that of compulsive disorder accompanied by hypochondriacal symptoms which are the body's negative way of making itself felt.

3

Jung's Major Practical Contributions

Jung's practical contributions evolved out of his own approach to the analytic process which for him consisted essentially in a dialogue and a mutuality requiring the emotional involvement of the analyst for change to occur. In recent times, psychoanalysis has also begun to address the importance of the subjectivity of the analyst for the analytic work. The Jungian techniques elaborated in this chapter are mostly those specifically discovered by Jung himself, although it has to be said that many Jungian practitioners have turned to clinical techniques from psychoanalysis to provide insights into pathological states such as denial, resistance, defences, acting-out, enactment, attacks on linking, projection, projective identification, reverie and above all, transference and countertransference and have integrated these into their clinical practice.

Those who incorporate the clinical with the mythological and remain in the tension between the two find that it is creative in their analytic work. For other practitioners it is experienced as a mythological/clinical split and it is along this fault line that the splits in the Jungian world have occurred.

In setting up the analytic contract with a patient or analysand, Jungian practitioners follow the same procedure used by psychoanalysts from other schools. Frequency of sessions per week, the possible duration of the therapy and the fee are discussed and agreed on in the initial session. Some Jungian practitioners favour the chair over the couch for the patient's use, as Jung himself did. However, many use either the couch or chair depending on the individual patient's perceived requirements at the time of starting therapy.

Some of Jung's specific contributions to practice include: *amplification*, his concept of *archetypal* transference/countertransference, *active imagination* and dream analysis. These will be elaborated further in what follows.

Amplification

As has already been pointed out, Jung was inspired by Frank
Miller's raw material to go on and develop many of his own ideas.
One of these, amplification, is a way of connecting the content from
a dream or fantasy with universal imagery by way of using
mythical, historical and cultural analogies. Jung takes the title and
related content of a poem of Frank Miller's, 'The Moth to the Sun',
and amplifies it to bring out its metaphorical meaning.

Jung states that in this poem God becomes the sun, which is a
perfect representation for divinity with its polarized beneficent life-
giving powers counter-balanced by its destructive ones. For this
reason, its zodiacal manifestation is the lion, which Samson killed to
free the parched earth from its scorching rays. This powerful force,
the libido, is the driving strength of the soul, which may be diverted
into either creative or destructive acts.

Jung then looks to the Upanishads and the Persian sun-god
Mithra to amplify his theme. One quote from the Upanishads goes
as follows:

> The Man of the size of a thumb, resides in the midst within the self, of
> the past and future, the Lord.
> The Man of the size of a thumb like flame free from smoke, of past and
> of Future the Lord, the same is today, tomorrow the same will He be.

Tom Thumb then represents the phallic symbol of the libido which
is also found in Goethe's *Faust* (1951 abridged version):

> *Mephistopheles*: I'll praise thee ere we separate: I see Thou knowest the
>   devil thoroughly: Here take this Key.
> *Faust*: That little thing!
> *Mephistopheles*: Take hold of it, not undervaluing!
> *Faust*: It glows, it shines, increases in my hand!
> *Mephistopheles*: How much it is worth, thou soon shalt understand, The
>   key will scent the true place from all others! Follow it down! – 'twill
>   lead thee to the Mothers!

At the beginning of the drama the devil, in the form of the black
dog, says the following: 'Part of that power, not understood, Which
always wills the bad and always creates the good.' This paradox is
at the heart of Jung's approach and he often quotes it to support his
contention that without evil nothing can be created.

The phallus is the symbolic representative of universal creative
power and many of the creatures that personify this power wear the
phallic pointed hat that denotes it. These include dwarves, Attis (the
earlier manifestation of Christ), and Mithra. The dwarf form con-
jures up the idea of the eternal youth, the personification of the
creative impulse in Jungian psychology. Jung continues to amplify

in this vein until he ends by linking the term libido, in its broadest sense, to Schopenhauer's meaning of Will. The highest expression of libido used in this way in human form is in the manifestation of the religious hero.

Returning to the myth of Pramantha, touched on in the previous chapter, which denotes the phallus that bores rhythmically into the opening in the feminine wood to produce the resulting fire, Agni, which is the offspring of this sexualized symbolic act of fire production. What Jung is trying to show here is the link both to what the patient was doing unconsciously but also to a universal phenomenon of the discovery of fire through sublimation of sexualized libido.

Jung links this sexualized libido with the libido from the presexual stage of the infant's development which, as we saw above, is different for him to Freud's autoerotic stage. The presexual stage for Jung is the nutritional stage and it is the regression to the presexual psychological stage that combines with the sexualized libido to produce the ancient symbols of agriculture.

> In the work of agriculture hunger and incest intermingle. The ancient cults of mother earth and all the superstitions founded thereon saw in the cultivation of the earth the fertilization of the mother. The aim of the action is desexualized, however, for it is the fruit of the field and the nourishment contained therein. The regression resulting from the incest prohibition leads, in this case, to the new valuation of the mother; this time, however, not as a sexual object, but as a nourisher. (Jung, 1991: 152)

In the case of the production of fire, Jung again points to the regression back to the presexual stage, in particular to the displaced rhythmic activity. As we saw, he relates the latter to masturbation or onanism, and the conclusion he arrives at is that fire production was originally an act of quasi-onanistic activity.

Similarly with the development of human speech, Jung traces its origins to a regression to the presexual stage where it turns to the external world to find an outlet. In the Upanishads, speech is called a light and related to the light of the Atman, the creative psychic force or libido. In this way, speech and fire may be seen as the first human arts that have resulted from the transformation of libido.

Both Agni and Christ are the ones who are sacrificed and who leave their redeeming fluids behind. With Christ it is his redeeming blood; with Agni it is the Soma, the holy drink of immortality. Both these link back to the presexualized libido of the presexualized nutritional stage. Christ's body and blood are ingested and the Soma is seen as the nourishing drink. The link back to the nutritional stage is why so many myths depict gods being devoured.

Jung links the sexualized libido that produces fire through rhythmic activity to onanism. The latter activity is a way of protecting the perpetrator from being involved in life because through onanism the greatest magic of sexual gratification lies within one's own power. In this way, one does not have to conquer sexual desire through wrestling with reality.

> Aladdin rubs his lamp and the obedient genii stand at his bidding; thus the fairy tale expresses the great psychologic advantage of the easy regression to the local sexual satisfaction. Aladdin's symbol subtly confirms the ambiguity of the magic fire preparation. (Jung, 1991: 166)

Jung relates this to the case of the peasant boy who was an incendiary. He was caught because it was noticed once that he was masturbating while watching the latest of his conflagrations. Although the preparation of fire has become an ordinary everyday activity, there is still the ceremonial preparation of fire which is hedged about with ritual activity. There are different ways of responding to the psychological regression that lies between the acting-out of a sterile onanism or the alternative, which is the path of sublimation.

The 'Analytic Third'

As can be seen from the above, the traditional usage of amplification as a technique takes the object as its starting point and then enlarges on it by way of mythological motifs. In a recent paper written by the American analytical psychologist, Joe Cambray, amplification has been rethought to take in its evolving role in analysis incorporating subjective and objective aspects of the amplifactory process (Cambray, 2000). Jung himself said: 'If I wish to treat another individual psychologically at all, I must for better or worse give up all pretensions to superior knowledge, all authority and desire to influence. I must perforce adopt a dialectical procedure consisting in a comparison of our mutual findings' (Jung, 1954: 5).

The use of the term 'subjective' traditionally applied to the patient's subjectivity in contributing personal and dream contents in a session. Cambray explores instead the analyst's subjectivity in using the amplifications that come to mind during a session. In *Symbols of Transformation*, Jung was seeking to locate himself in what he called 'my myth' through which he became linked to a profound sense of self. 'Thus the subjectivity of this "my myth" attitude is inextricably linked to a reified, perhaps somewhat autistic self, rather than a post-modern self emerging out of the play of psychological processes. The latter is more in accord with the inescapable subjectivity of the analyst in relation to the reality of an other' (Cambray, 2000: 13).

Cambray advocates sparing use of the analyst's internal amplifications rather than silence or transference interpretations when a patient is curious about those. It is vital to guard against over-indulgence on the part of the analyst in airing their internal processes as this can lead to narcissistic displays with corresponding envious feelings on the part of the patient. The need for a combined analyst/analysand narrative in the amplicatory process arises in the interactive field between the two and can give rise to the 'analytic third' which is constellated between the two in the interactive field that exists between them and is not entirely the analyst nor entirely the analysand. These concepts are explored more fully in the section below that deals with Schwartz-Salant's *Archetypal Foundations of Projective Identification*.

The exploration through amplification of the myths embedded in both the analyand's, as well as the analyst's, psyche ultimately (*teleologically*) emanates from the 'analytic third'. 'Amplification, in this light, can be re-presented as an unfolding of the objective psyche as it plays through our diverse subjectivities' (Cambray, 2000: 20).

Cambray illustrates the shared amplificatory discourse with the following piece of case material that took place just before a break. The patient was a psychologically sophisticated entrepreneur who had recently been diagnosed as suffering from an untreatable, chronic, debilitating illness and this was 'casting a pall over the analytic work'. The symbolic and relational aspects of his psychosomatic illness were looked at analytically but this did nothing to alleviate his despair. As a result of the analyst's reverie and amplification, the countervailing theme of 'hope' becomes important as we shall see.

> My own reveries as we entered this impasse led me back to a memory of a childhood illllness that similarly had been poorly understood and to how I had had to try and manage my mother's anxieties, as well as my own, especially around visits to the family physician. I recalled a coping strategy from that period in which reading myths played a prominent role. These had provided containing images for my distress, and heroic figures I could identify with to counter the ills. Pursuing these memories of the discomfort in having to supply hope then led me to remember the tale of Pandora. (Cambray, 2000: 23)

Briefly, the myth of Pandora stems from Zeus's planned retaliation for the theft by Prometheus of fire from the gods to give to human-kind. She is fashioned into a desirable woman from earth and water and bestowed with desirable attributes to make her even more alluring. She was brought to earth along with a great sealed jar and first offered to Prometheus, who was too canny to be seduced. Epimetheus, however, is easily taken in and eagerly accepts her. When Pandora opened the sealed jar, all the ills that beset humanity were released leaving only hope behind.

The accessing of this myth in response to the anger and despair directly related to illness and absence experienced by the 'analytic third' led Cambray to share it too quickly with the patient, who scornfully dismissed it. The analyst had Pandora-like spilled the contents of his mind into the session and the patient's scornful reaction was a form of projective identification that inhibited the analyst's capacity for symbolic play. Instead, he became embarrassed. The analyst's sharing at the moment that he did so had been inappropriately timed and was experienced by the patient as trying to shift the emphasis too quickly from the complexed interactive field, in which the 'analytic third' was caught, to the symbolic field. The Pandora amplification accessing hope was tactless, even though accurate, as it proved unbearable for the patient at that moment.

As a result of this insight, the analyst was able to empathize with the emotional suffering the patient was trapped in and this resulted in a more secure alliance and 'deeper exploration of the analysand's schizoid defenses (as well as my own) became possible' (Cambray, 2000: 25).

Archetypal Transference and Countertransference

The importance of alchemy for Jung in establishing an historical precedent for his approach to psychology has already been written about above. The principal goal the two had in common was the extracting of gold from base metals, although this was, of course, symbolic in the more sophisticated alchemical work as it was in the psychological. This section will illustrate how Jung applied alchemy in practice with regard to its use in archetypal transference and countertransference. Jung had ambivalent views about transference and at one time called it the alpha and omega of the analytical method. At others, he talks of its importance as relative, for instance, where he says: 'I personally am always glad when there is only a mild transference or when it is practically unnoticeable' (Jung, 1954: 172).

However, this was not the case when it came to a powerfully erotic instance of it and Carotenuto, in his book *A Secret Symmetry*, claims that it was Jung's own experience of this in his work with Sabina Speilrein that led to his writing about it many years later in *The Psychology of the Transference* (Carotenuto, 1982).

Some of the concepts from alchemy have already been touched on above, for instance, the *coniunctio*. This referred to the idea of the mystic or higher marriage which has two sources in alchemy: one Christian, the other pagan. The Christian denotes the union of Christ and the Church; the pagan that of the marriage of the mystic with God.

The image of the coniunctio has an archetypal basis in the unconscious and it is this imagery that can become activated in an in-depth analysis. According to Jung, the analyst and the analysand are both equally in the work and will thus be equally affected by the unconscious processes they encounter. Jung used the image of the alchemical vessel to denote the analytical container in which the transformation of the two takes place. This is why individuals in Jungian analysis often talk of analysing 'with' someone rather than being analysed 'by' them.

Dreams may signal the onset of an archetypal transference in producing the kind of symbolism that is associated with a conjoining or coming together of opposite forces. Examples of this would be a dove, the classical symbol of reconciliation, or a winged serpent, denoting the symbolic union of above with below.

The sort of psychic energy that becomes activated between analyst and analysand at this time is experienced as having a mercurial, even impish or diabolical quality. In alchemy, this was personified as Hermes or Mercurius – the patron god of both alchemy and analysis. Jung came to call this figure the *Trickster*, and it is everywhere and at all times active in human doings which is why one is always saying and doing foolish things which, with a little foresight, could be avoided. It also explains why millions of people can get caught in mass cults like that of Nazism and why Pythagoras could not set up, once and for all, the rule of wisdom, or Christianity the Kingdom of Heaven on Earth.

As the patron god of both alchemy and analysis, the Trickster is to be found at work in alchemical texts that at times describe in astonishing detail the sort of phenomenology that can be observed in the analysis of unconscious processes. Jung turned to one, the *Rosarium*, to shed light on archetypal transference/countertransference phenomena in the analytical situation. This is a medieval text illustrated with drawings of a royal couple dating from 1550 for as Jung says: 'These curiosities of the Middle Ages contain the seeds of much that emerged in clearer form only many centuries later' (Jung, 1954: 201).

The Rosarium
The idea of the quaternity is a universal phenomenon denoting the idea of wholeness that is central to alchemy. There are the four

seasons, four elements, four primary colours and four psychological orientations as explored above under psychological types. The whole work of *Faust* revolves around Goethe's life-long search for the fourth function, thinking, which was his inferior one. In the same way, what some of the more perceptive alchemists were in quest of was the 'gold' that was to be found through contacting the inferior function buried deep in the unconscious. For Jung, the alchemical quest was akin to the central goal of analysis which he came to call *individuation* and the integration of the 'inferior' fourth function into consciousness is one of the major tasks of individuation.

As the illustrations are an important part of *Rosarium*, I will paint word pictures of the relevant ones. If the reader wishes to look at them, they are in Volume 16, *The Practice of Psychotherapy*, in the chapter entitled *The Psychology of the Transference*. They are also to be found in Nathan Schwartz-Salant's (1989) *The Borderline Personality*, which is dealt with in the next section and in Elie Humbert's (1984) *C.G. Jung*, in the section after that. Picture 1 of the text is of the mercurial fountain and contains much alchemical symbolism: the sun and moon as opposites; the four elements depicted by four stars; and the fountain or vessel wherein the transformation takes place. The uprising and flowing back of the water in the mercurial fountain characterizes Mercurius as the serpent endlessly fertilizing and devouring itself until it gives birth to itself again.

Picture 2 brings in the element of incest that is an essential component of the archetypal transference and countertransference. The King and Queen, bridegroom and bride, are depicted as standing on the sun and moon pointing to the incestuous brother-sister relationship of Apollo and Diana. Sun and moon in alchemical texts are called *Sol* and *Luna* and this more mature model took the place of Jung's early division of *Logos* (differentiatedness) and *Eros* (relatedness). The incestuous nature of the relationship depicted in the picture is emphasized further by the left-handed contact between the two – that is from the sinister or unconscious side. Further associations with the left side are to do with the heart which is related to love but also with all the moral contradictions that are connected with affective states.

This left-sided contact in the picture indicates the dubious nature of the relationship, which is a mixture of heavenly and earthly love with the added ingredient of incestuous love. The couple are holding a device of two flowers each in their right hands which criss-cross each other. These are further crossed at their meeting point from above by a flower held in the beak of a dove.

The incest that is portrayed here is a central characteristic of the alchemical and the analytical work. It must be emphasized here that Jung is not advocating actual incest but, instead, is pointing to the symbolic kind which was also portrayed in *Symbols of Transformation*. What he is actually getting at is that individuating, becoming one's own person, entails a symbolic re-entry into mother, that is, a regression back to the incestuous relationship in order to be reborn. Symbolic incest, therefore, represents a coming together with one's own being, a union of like with like which is why it exerts an unholy fascination – as we know from the all-too-frequent occurrences of it in ordinary life.

In much the same way, a powerful 'incestuous' attraction may be activated between analyst and analysand when the archetypal processes come into play during the course of an in-depth analysis. The criss-crossing remarked on above is now revealed in the pattern of relationship that comes into play between the analyst and the analysand. The energy can flow in a variety of directions but does not usually do so at the same time. However, there may arise times during the course of an in-depth analysis when all the energy channels are active simultaneously, which leads to massive confusion. These are the times when the relationship is in danger of breaking down or of being acted-out in some way.

One path that is open between the two is the uncomplicated personal relationship. Another is the relationship of each to their *anima/animus*, also known as the *syzygy*, lying in the unconscious. The animus is the archetypal active principle and the anima the archetypal passive one. In Jung's 'classical' theory, the animus belonged in the woman's unconscious and the anima in the man's. More-recent thinking has revised this to incorporate the yoked syzygy equally into male and female unconsciousness.

The next path of relationship is between the yoked anima/animus of each to the other. Lastly, there can be a one-sided projection onto the analyst of the woman's animus or of the man's anima when the conscious attitude is identical with animus or anima. This may activate a corresponding counter-projection on the part of the analyst so that the two are then caught in an anima/animus projection onto each other which usually results in an acting-out of some sort. The acting-out may at this point take the form of a sexual relationship and, as it is of a deeply unconscious kind, it would be tinged with unresolved incestuous impulses.

Jung went on to call this kind of incestuous attraction *kinship libido* and it is ultimately through the spiritualization of this incestuous libido that the psychological alchemical work comes to its fruition in the constellation of the coniunctio and the birth of the divine child, which is individuation.

Picture 3 of the *Rosarium* shows the King (Sol) and Queen (Luna) in naked confrontation with the dove once again between them. The text says: 'O Luna, let me be thy husband,' and Luna responds, 'O Sol, I must submit to thee' (Jung, 1954: 236). The eroticism of the picture is mediated by the dove both as a symbol of the soul which provides the relational aspect between the King (spirit) and the Queen (body). The psyche is then seen to be half spirit and half body.

Picture 4 depicts the two figures naked in the alchemical bath with the dove again between them. The psychology of this picture centres on a descent into the unconscious – a kind of 'night sea journey' – which is the path taken in all heroic myths leading to symbolic rebirth.

Picture 5, The Coniunctio, shows the pair in a passionate embrace enclosed by the water and they have returned to the chaotic beginnings. At first sight it looks as if instinct has triumphed but the psychology of the coniunctio is not so simple. The union depicted here denotes the symbolic union of opposites and in this way instinctive energy is transformed into symbolical activity. The dove, the uniting symbol, has disappeared as the pair themselves have become symbolic.

Picture 6 shows the death or *nigredo* stage that follows on from the coniunctio as once the opposites unite the flow of energy ceases. Death means the extinction of consciousness and the stagnation of psychic life. The two are united in one body but with two heads. 'The situation described in our picture is a kind of Ash Wednesday' (Jung, 1954: 260). This annual lamentation which takes place in many cultures corresponds to an archetypal or typical event. This is linked to the incestuous theme which runs through the whole of the *Rosarium* in the following way. The difficult dilemma that anyone undertaking a confrontation with the unconscious is faced is that nature will be mortified either way because to commit incest goes against nature but equally so does not yielding to ardent desire. With the integration into the ego of the powerful contents in the unconscious there results an inevitable inflation which has a serious impact on the ego which may be experienced as a death.

Picture 7 shows the soul mounting to heaven out of the decaying unified body of the King and Queen. This corresponds psychologically to a dark state of disorientation and the collapse of ego-consciousness. When the ego is overwhelmed by unconscious contents this is experienced as a loss of soul – the dark night of the soul that is depicted in the writings of St. John of the Cross.

Picture 8 shows the dead couple being sprinkled on by falling dew from heaven. The previous stage of the darkness of death when the union of opposites reaches its nadir now begins to lighten. This is what Jung calls an *enantiodromia*, the psychological law touched on above which was discovered by Heraclitus where everything eventually transforms into its opposite. This law underwrites Jung's concepts of the self-regulating power of the psyche and of *compensation*.

Picture 9 shows the soul returning from heaven and unifying with the purified body. It is this unification which is the goal of the perceptive alchemists and depth-psychologists alike – in the latter case it is the freeing of ego-consciousness from contamination with the unconscious. Just as relationship is at the centre of the alchemical transformation so, too, in analysis it is the relationship between analyst and analysand that effects the transformation of both.

Picture 10 shows the birth of the *androgyne*, the symbol of wholeness, with the right side of the body being male and the left female. This signifies that the individual has reached the stage of consciousness where the opposites represented by Sol and Luna are held in balance. This is different to the earlier figure of the *hermaphrodite* which is the state of primordial union. In Picture 10, the *androgyne* stands on the moon – the feminine principle – and holds a snake depicting the principle of evil which is connected with the work of redemption. This section will conclude with a quote from the text of the *Rosarium*:

> It is manifest, therefore, that the stone is the master of the philosophers, as if he (the philosopher) were to say that he does of his own nature that which he is compelled to do; and so the philosopher is not the master, but rather the minister, of the stone. (Jung, 1954: 313)

The androgyne symbolizes nothing less than the philosopher's stone or individuation and is the end result of a slow process of analysis during which the libido is extracted from the alluring fascination of the eroticized transference/countertransference.

The two sections below will flesh out the above with clinical approaches to the alchemical text of the *Rosarium*.

Archetypal Foundations of Projective Identification

The American analytical psychologist, Nathan Schwartz-Salant, has related the alchemical imagery of the *Psychology of the Transference* to Klein's concept of *projective identification*, both of which appeared in 1946 (Schwartz-Salant, 1989). They met with very different receptions: Klein's work had an electrifying effect on many psychoanalysts, while Jung's was seen as too abstract, even by analytical psychologists, to be useful in clinicial work.

As this paper uses projective identification as its central motif, it would be as well to say a few words about it. It is an unconscious way of interacting with another which is often accompanied by feelings of confusion and panic but there is another aspect to it as Rosemary Gordon (in Schwartz-Salant, 1989) has pointed out: it has the power to break down boundaries. These include inner psychic boundaries, as well as those between self and others. Jung uses several terms which equate with projective identification: 'unconscious identity'; 'psychic infection'; 'participation mystique'; and 'feeling-into'.

As with everything in Jung, there is always a positive as well as a negative aspect to anything and he was interested in the creative/ destructive possibilities that were inherent in projective identification. Schwartz-Salant relates this to Jung's work based on the *Rosarium*, which was the latter's Ariadne's thread that led him through the complexities of the transference.

The dominant image in this work is of the hermaphrodite linking aspects between opposites. Both the positive and negative aspects of the hermaphrodite are experienced in projective identification, for example, the harmonious linking of opposites leads to complementary aspects of a process. On the other hand, conflicting opposites lead to the chaotic states – fusion and splitting – of projective identification experienced in borderline states of mind.

In the *Psychology of the Transference*, Jung proposes that the phenomenology of participation mystique activates the archetypal transference. Schwartz-Salant claims that Jung's alchemical speculations addressed processes in what he calls the *subtle body* area which is akin to Winnicott's concept of *transitional space*. This space is not located inside, outside or between people but to a 'third' area whose processes can only be perceived by the eye of the imagination. This lies in an interactive field structured by images that have a strong effect on the conscious personality. Projective identification is directed to the transformation of processes in this third area.

Identifying it is crucial in the initiating of the alchemical opus, for instance in getting into the *prima materia* or unconscious or in arriving at the *nigredo*. The therapist must be able to maintain sufficient emotional distance from the powerful feelings that are engendered in him by the borderline patient otherwise the former will continue to be manipulated into enacting the latter's fantasies. The strong affects that may be engendered in this way include boredom, fury, avoidance and anxiety.

Schwartz-Salant gives an example of what it feels like to be the 'container' for contents projected into it. A male patient was having a conversation with him when he stopped suddenly at a point where it would have been more natural for him to continue talking. At the same time, the patient behaved as if nothing were wrong. After a while it became clear that each was waiting for the other to say something. This became gradually more painful until the therapist felt impelled to bridge the intolerable tension.

The reason for the powerful feelings in this period was the result of the patient's projective identification which was putting his blank mind into the therapist: 'He was easing this "absence", encased in a paranoid shell, into me, then watching me in hope that I would somehow return to him his (functioning) mind . . . when I disengaged and ended the encounter, the patient grew angry' (Schwartz-Salant, 1989: 102).

The alchemical model moves the therapist out of the sphere of having to know it all by the discovery of the 'unconscious couple'. The process causes the two parties to get involved in transforming the third, which is Mercurius, and in this way to be transformed themselves.

As was shown above, the early pictures depict dangerous fusion/splitting states. The alchemical process offers the possibility of transforming negative projective identification of this kind into a more positive outcome without undervaluing its dark, chaotic aspect. At the height of feelings of dissociation on the part of the analyst and analysand as portrayed in Picture 7, a mystery at the interactive level is being enacted and the soul is ascending toward a state of union with the transcendent self.

When the higher marriage between analyst and analysand begins to feel more stable, positive experiences of the hermaphrodite begin to emerge to create a linking quality between the two that is the source of the therapeutic alliance which is crucial to the work with borderline patients. The unified self that is constellated becomes the generator of shared experiences which are the proper goal of projective identification.

The Alchemical Process
The French analytical psychologist, Elie Humbert, has written an accessible book on Jung's work entitled *C.G. Jung*. One chapter of the book is about the transference as elaborated by Jung through the *Rosarium* text. Although transference/countertransference projections are an everyday part of living, the clinical version offers the possibility for both therapist and patient to make these projections more conscious and in that way to reclaim them as part of oneself.

In common with Jung and Schwartz-Salant, Humbert reiterates that the way to enable this to happen is through relationship which is why an individual would find it impossible to analyse themselves through reading a book. Mere abstract knowledge will not enable the necessary unconscious processes to become active that are needed for psychological growth. This psychotherapeutic relationship, for Jung, is founded on 'psychic contagion':

> The patient, by bringing an activated unconscious content to bear upon the doctor, constellates the corresponding unconscious material in him, owing to the inductive effect which always emanates from projections in greater or lesser degree. (Jung, 1954: 176)

For Humbert, what Jung means by 'psychic contagion' refers to the countertransference and a state of mutual unconsciousness is essential in the analytic relationship. There are obvious dangers in this and both may become fixed in the eroticized component of the transference/countertransference when the mutual demand for actual physical intimacy becomes overwhelming. There are various typical responses to this state on the part of the analyst and if the latter becomes caught in any of them it is likely to lead to acting-out of one sort or another.

Powerful anxiety feelings is one response on the part of the analyst who feels out of their depth and this can result in a defensive admonitory way of dealing with the patient. One actual incident I know of was of a male analyst saying to a woman patient: 'I am not Jung and you're not Toni Wolff!' This kind of stern acting-out of the countertransference is potentially destructive of the analytic work and an analysis may break down at this point. The opposite response is a mutual 'falling into' the erotic feelings culminating in an actual affair.

As we saw in Jung's elaboration of the *Rosarium* incest is the underlying motif of both that text and of the analytical relationship. This needs to be contained and not acted-out so that it may eventually culminate in the *Hieros gamos* or endogamous marriage. Jung took the terms 'endogamy' and 'exogamy' from anthropology and they apply in the first instance to marriage within the kinship group and in the second to marriage outside of it. Jung applied these terms to his two models of marriage – one the spiritual/psychological one, the other the outer/legal one.

The incestuous feelings experienced in the analytical relationship draw their power *teleologically* from the goal in analysis of bringing consciousness back to its unconscious sources. As we saw from Jung's treatment of the alchemical text, what interested him was the analogy between the royal couple depicted there and the unconscious process that develops between analyst and analysand which generate the multiple relationships that can arise between the two.

Pictures 3 and 4 show the King and Queen naked and Humbert interprets this to mean that the honeymoon phase of the analysis is over and that *shadow* contents are beginning to be constellated in the analytic relationship.

> But it happens eventually that analysts make a mistake: an error, a forgetful moment, a lapse, they stumble – a small thing perhaps, yet their shadow appears. This is a moment of truth. (Humbert, 1984: 75)

The analysis may break down at this point because the analysand may feel either critical of the analyst for not being perfect or released from a transference coloured by the fantasy of the 'all-knowing one'. This may be as far as an individual analysand needs to go as it enables the person to live more authentically.

Picture 5 shows the couple having intercourse, which figuratively points to them uniting in the quest for greater consciousness. This is followed by the depression generated by the inhibition of the incestuous longings. The long process of death – depression – and purification has now been embarked on. This is a long initiation that involves psychological death leading eventually to rebirth and in tribal cultures is accompanied by instructing of the initiate by the elders as to what they are experiencing. The analyst must now be wary of succumbing to this way of dealing with the patient's feelings of anguish and despair during this initiatory period as the analysis could then degenerate into a purely intellectual or spiritual exercise.

In Picture 9 the figure of the androgyne, the psychologically more evolved figure to the earlier one of the hermaphrodite, is shown now in a purified state as the soul returns to join with it. The importance of the androgynous figure is that it symbolizes the true realization for the analysand that what has been looked for on the outer level in a partner or the analyst is now found *within* where it truly belongs. The resolution of transference/countertransference feelings is now well on the way as the energy constellated has been used up. The end result is the ability on the part of both to walk away from the analytic work with mutual feelings of wellbeing and satisfaction. An analysis that is aborted has a deleterious impact on both parties as an in-depth analysis involves a lengthy investment of time and energy and the ability of the analyst and analysand to withstand the rigours that are a part of the process.

Humbert says that Picture 10 depicting the new birth through the royal marriage shows the androgynous two-headed figure wearing two crowns. The new birth has come about through the relationship between the ego and the self which engenders the symbolic function. The capacity for symbolization is the fount of all creativity and it is the realization of this through the conjunction of opposites that Jung saw as 'the principle of humanization at work' (Humbert, 1984: 81).

An important point to bear in mind about Jungian analysis is that its true goal is not narcissistic self-absorption for the length of its duration but the continuing investment in relationships with others. 'The unrelated human being lacks wholeness, for he can achieve wholeness only through the soul, and the soul cannot exist without its other side, which is always found in a "You"' (Jung, 1954: 244).

Active Imagination

Jung's writing on the *transcendent function* has been touched on already in the first Chapter and is closely allied to the use of active imagination so that a description of the former is necessary before going on to delineate the latter. Jung first wrote his paper on the transcendent function in 1916 and it remained unpublished until it was discovered many years later by students of the C.G. Jung Institute in Zurich. Jung revised it in 1958, 42 years after he had first tackled the subject.

In this paper, Jung is attempting to show how coming to terms with the unconscious may be put into practice. He emphasizes yet again that this is a religious and moral undertaking not to be undertaken lightly as the subliminal contents of the psyche possess such a powerful charge that they can produce a psychosis when unleashed. 'For the unconscious is not this thing or that; it is the Unknown as it immediately affects us' (Jung, 1960b: 68).

He is also at pains to differentiate his *synthetic* approach from what he scathingly calls the *reductive* – the difference between the two will become clear as the contents of the paper unfold themselves.

The transcendent arises from the union of conscious and unconscious contents. He derived the term 'transcendent' from mathematics concerning the function of real and imaginary numbers. Just as consciousness is antithetical to the unconscious so it is simultaneously complementary to it and vice versa. Briefly, the unconscious contains all the fantasy and forgotten contents which have not yet risen above the threshold of consciousness and is also the realm of the inherited structuring constituents of the psyche – the archetypes. Consciousness, on the other hand, because of its directed way of functioning, exercises an inhibiting attitude to incompatible unconscious contents.

In order for civilization to evolve it was vital for humankind to develop a directed, well-functioning consciousness. This was accompanied by a repression of unconscious contents resulting in a one-sidedness due to the banishment of these from the conscious realm. However, unwelcome contents make themselves felt in a variety of ways, for instance, through dreams or slips of the tongue and, if the repression is extreme, in pathological symptoms.

Jung's answer to this is to advocate getting rid of the separation between conscious and unconscious. This may be accomplished through activating the transcendent function, which is composed of tendencies from both realms. This may be constellated by a constructive or synthetic analytic approach where the analyst is aware of the potential of the transcendent function. In this way, the analyst mediates the transcendent function for the patient, helping to bring the conscious and unconscious together to arrive at a new attitude.

The synthetic approach, according to Jung, is the one that values symbolic meaning in dream images or fantasies in their own right rather than reducing them to being caused by something in the individual's childhood. In this way, unconscious phenomena are regarded as if they had intention and purpose (teleology) pointing to future psychological development. The consequence of this approach for the analytical relationship is that everything emanating from the patient should not be regarded as historically true but as subjectively so. For instance, the erotic transference may be seen historically as infantile but its true significance, according to Jung, lay not in its historical antecedents but in its purpose. The symbolic meaning in the erotic transference as explored above in the section on the *Rosarium* is what needs to be made conscious. 'The word "symbol" being taken to mean the best possible expression for a complex fact not yet clearly apprehended by consciousness' (Jung, 1960b: 75). Jung's intention in activating the transcendent function is to gain access to the self-regulating function of the psyche, which he sees as having been inhibited by critical attention and the directed will. As the unconscious loses its regulating influence it has an intensifying effect on conscious processes as energy that is repressed builds up a charge that may then explode. Jung cites Nietzsche as an example of this:

> Thus the regulating influence is suppressed, but not the secret counter-action of the unconscious, which from now on becomes clearly noticeable in Nietzsche's writings. First he seeks his adversary in Wagner, whom he cannot forgive for *Parsifal*, but soon his whole wrath turns against Christianity and in particular against St. Paul, who in some ways suffered a fate similar to Nietzsche's . . . (whose) psychosis first produced an identification with the 'Crucified Christ' and then with the dismembered Dionysus. (Jung, 1960b: 80)

Knowledge of the regulating influence of the psyche can prevent much bad experience and so gaining access to this knowledge is a necessary part of healthy living. Jung illustrates the way to gain access to this and says that the intensity of any emotional disturbance is where the actual value lies – for it is the energy that is caught up in this which needs to be released for it to be at the individual's disposal. However, this cannot be done intellectually.

The way to realize the transcendent function is to gain access to unconscious material and Jung points to various ways of doing this. He calls this process *active imagination*, which is the collaboration of the conscious and unconscious mind in order to facilitate the emergence of those contents that lie just below the threshold of consciousness. The co-operation of a strong ego is absolutely central to this process as it is not without its dangers, the most serious of which is the possible possession of the conscious mind by unconscious contents which can result in a psychotic episode.

The starting point of active imagination must always be the emotional state and becoming as conscious as possible of the mood that is around is vital. One way of accessing this is through writing down without reservation any fantasies as they occur.

Another is through painting or drawing and individuals who possess some talent in this direction can give expression to their mood by visualizing it. In this way something is created which is influenced by both conscious and unconscious, giving the former an outlet in its striving for substance and the latter in its striving for the light of awareness. Other possible methods that may be helpful are working with plastic materials, body movement and automatic writing (see above).

> The whole procedure is a kind of enrichment and clarification of the affect, whereby the affect and its contents are brought nearer to consciousness, becoming at the same time more impressive and more understandable . . . it creates a new situation, since the previously unrelated affect has become a more or less clear and articulate idea, thanks to the assistance and co-operation of the conscious mind. This is the beginning of the transcendent function i.e. of the collaboration of conscious and unconscious data. (Jung, 1960b: 82)

All critical attention must be suspended and an attitude of expectation be engendered instead. Also, it is important to guard against being seduced by the intellect, on the one hand, or by an over-valuing of the aesthetic content, on the other. The latter can lead to an ego-orientated attempt to create pretty pictures. Vigilance is required at all times during this process as it is easy for the conscious attitude to predominate with its greater familiarity and clearer formulations. Feeling-toned contents are far less comfortable to deal with.

Jung goes on to make the all-important point that a capacity for inner dialogue is essential in enabling outer dialogue which pre-supposes an acceptance of the validity of other points of view. 'For, to the degree that he does not admit the validity of the other person, he denies the 'other' within himself the right to exist – and vice versa' (Jung, 1960b: 89).

Dream Analysis

Jung held dreams to be of the highest importance in portraying messages from the unconscious to consciousness and we saw above how each turning point in his own life was preceded by a significant dream.

Similarly, dreams play a central role in Jungian analysis and some analyses are based almost entirely on working with dream material. I see patients and analysands from other parts of the world and they often ask for a 'dream analysis'. In my experience, this involves the patient bringing a written account of the dreams immediately preceding the analytic session. Sometimes a copy of this is given to the analyst and the two work on it together. I find this as creative a way of conducting analysis as any other as long as the sessions do not become flooded with dream images, which can easily be used defensively by the patient to prevent any in-depth analysis taking place. I usually find, instead, that it is possible to detect recurring motifs in any dream series and identifying these opens up the way to working with the patient's resistance and defences, as well as, work in the transference.

Examples of some recurring dream images are: anxiety feelings; feelings of inadequacy; sexual themes that reveal the patient's sexual frustration or over indulgence; parental complexes; abnormal fear of illness or death; violent affect or the opposite which manifests as a lack of concern in situations where this would be aberrant. The following brief quote summarizes Jung's view of dreaming (Jung's italics): '. . . the dream is a *spontaneous self-portrayal, in symbolic form, of the actual situation in the unconscious*' (Jung, 1960b: 263).

Dreams have always exercised a fascination for humankind which is related to the strangeness of their content and origin. 'They do not arise, like other conscious contents, from any clearly discernible, logical and emotional continuity of experience, but are remnants of a peculiar psychic activity taking place during sleep' (Jung, 1960b: 237). Their ubiquitous fascination may also lie in the fact that they were phylogenetically an older mode of thinking as Nietzsche suggests.

At first sight the contents may appear unrelated to anything in conscious experience but further exploration will show that some of them have their origin in the recent past.

Another aspect of dreams is their capacity to point the way forward. 'We know . . . that every psychic structure, regarded from the final standpoint, has its own peculiar meaning and purpose in the actual psychic process. This criterion must also be applied to dreams' (Jung, 1960b: 240).

Finality

To exemplify his hypothesis of *finality* Jung presents the following dream with accompanying associations to it: 'I was standing in a strange garden and picked an apple from a tree. I looked about cautiously, to make sure that no one saw me' (Jung, 1960b: 241). The above was the dream of a young man who associated to it in this way. As a boy he had stolen pears from a neighbour's garden. The bad conscience left over from that act is evident in the dream and reminded him of an experience from the previous day. On this occasion he had encountered a young woman who was a casual acquaintance and they had exchanged a few words. At that moment a man passed by whom he knew and he was aware of a sudden feeling of embarrassment as if he knew he was doing something wrong.

The apple in the dream reminded him of the one in the Garden of Eden and he had never come to terms with the fact that the eating of it had such dire consequences for the first parents. It made him feel angry with God who was punishing humankind for the qualities he had instilled in them in the first place. His further association with this was that his father had sometimes punished him for things that he found incomprehensible. One of these, for which he sustained the worst punishment, was secretly watching girls bathe. This finally led to the revelation that he had recently begun a liaison (as yet unconsummated) with a housemaid and had a meeting with her on the evening before the dream.

The erotic associations with the dream are fairly obviously accompanied by the feeling of bad conscience so that the linking theme becomes one of *guilt*. It is vital to take these two components together in order to arrive at the purpose of the dream which is to bring into greater awareness for the dreamer that he has unconscious guilt feelings about erotic events. It is he himself who is judging his conduct as reprehensible although consciously he appears to think that there is nothing wrong in what he is doing as all his friends are doing the same thing.

Jung then explores the meaning of moral standards that have been handed down through the ages, particularly with regard to the strongest desires. The way that this collective inhibition relates to this particular young man and his associations to the content of his dream are to demonstrate to him the necessity of a moral standpoint which he is trying to deny.

In his conscious attitude, the young man denies that there are any moral consequences of his actions but 'man is a morally responsible being who, voluntarily or involuntarily, submits to the morality that he himself has created' (Jung, 1960b: 244). Here again we encounter the compensatory nature of the unconscious in opposing the conscious attitude. Jung refers to St. Augustine who said that he was glad that God did not hold him responsible for his dreams. This compensatory function is the reason why it is essential to know the individual's conscious situation at the moment of dreaming.

This deeply moral sense that permeates all Jung's work led to him being accused of stepping outside the realm of psychology and into that of theology as was stated above in the section devoted to Father Victor White. His response to this charge which he reiterated many times over is as follows:

> the moral order, nor the idea of God, nor any religion has dropped into man's lap from outside, straight down from heaven, as it were, but . . . he contains all this within himself, and for this reason can produce it all out of himself . . . The ideas of the moral order and of God belong to the ineradicable substrate of the human soul. That is why any honest psychology . . . must come to terms with these facts. (Jung, 1960b: 278)

Compensation

A compensatory dream of Nebuchadnezzar from the *Book of Daniel* while he was at the height of his power demonstrates the vital function of dreaming. The dream went as follows:

> I saw, and behold a tree in the midst of the earth, and the height thereof was great.
>
> The tree grew, and was strong, and the height thereof reached unto heaven, And the sight thereof to the end of all the earth.
>
> The leaves thereof were fair, and the fruit thereof much, and in it was meat for all: the beasts of the field had shadow under it, and the fowls of the heaven dwelt in the boughs thereof, and all flesh was fed of it.
>
> I saw in the visions of my head upon my bed, and behold, a watcher and a holy one came down from heaven;
>
> He cried aloud, and said thus, Hew down the tree, and cut off his branches, shake off his leaves, and scatter his fruit: let the beasts get away from under it, and the fowls from his branches.
>
> Nevertheless leave the stump of his roots in the earth, even with a band of iron and brass in the tender grass of the field; and let it be wet with the dew of heaven, and let his portion be with the beasts in the grass of the earth:

Let his heart be changed from man's, and let a beast's heart be given unto him; and let seven times pass over him. (Book of Daniel: 10–16 AV, in Jung, 1960b: 251)

The tree is, of course, Nebuchadnezzar himself and the dream is an attempt at compensating the megalomania of the king, who ended by becoming psychotic. This kind of dream may appear to anyone who has an over-weaning sense of their own value as they have risen outwardly beyond their capacity as an individual. In today's terms this is known as the Peter Principle, which is tellingly portrayed by Anthony Powell as the egregious fictional character, Widmerpool, in his series of novels 'A Dance to the Music of Time'.

It would be useful to give an example of the synthetic approach as described above in its application to dream analysis. An unmarried woman dreamt that someone gave her a wonderful richly orna-mented, antique sword dug up out of a tumulus. Her associations with it were that her father had once flashed his dagger in the sun in front of her which had left an abiding impression. He was a strong man of Celtic origin who had many amorous adventures. She associated the sword with a Celtic one as the dream sword had ancient runes carved on it. The sword was brought to light again out of the grave.

Jung's synthetic interpretation of the dream was that the patient was above all in need of such a weapon. She lived life passively with no driving will of her own unlike her father, who had it both literally and figuratively and had used it to live a full life. His weapon was a passionate, unbending will with which he made his way through life. She had not appreciated until the dream that she was her father's daughter and that his passionate will lay buried deep in her own unconscious.

Context

As the contents of all dreams are non-rational, representing frag-ments of involuntary psychic activity, Jung's policy when con-fronted with any dream was to admit to himself that he had no idea what it meant. The possible interpretations of any dream are innumerable so that the only way of arriving at a fitting inter-pretation is with the dreamer's associations and Jung developed a method which he called 'taking up the context'. He compared this with the deciphering of a difficult text and described it as consisting in taking up every salient point in the dream with the dreamer.

The following example of a dream – not easily understandable at first – was that of a young man. He was, at the time, engaged to a young woman from a 'good family' who consistently appeared in his dreams in an unflattering – even scandalous – light. Eventually, Jung concluded that despite the young man's conscious resistance, his unconscious portrayal of his fiancée in a negative manner meant something. The patient's neurosis had started shortly after his engagement and this, combined with the recurring dream messages, led Jung to persuade him to initiate enquiries. These confirmed the unflattering dream images and, when the patient discontinued the engagement, his neurosis receded.

Collective and Personal Dreams

Jung goes on to distinguish 'big' dreams from personal ones. The former are usually remembered throughout the dreamer's life and 'not infrequently prove to be the richest jewel in the treasure-house of psychic experience' (Jung, 1960b: 290). Big dreams are those that come from the realm of the collective unconscious and are archetypal in nature.

Jung says that these often occur as part of the individuation process and I would like to proffer one of mine that initiated me onto my own individuating path. This dream occurred many years ago and, although it is still important to me, it has lost its affective charge so that I have been able to use it in seminars with students and in other contexts. The dream happened at the end of my first analysis which lasted for four-and-a-half years at a frequency of three times a week. Towards the end of this analysis, my analyst encouraged me to think of training as a therapist, whereupon I applied to a training institute and was accepted on the strength of a brief interview. The reader will appreciate how many decades ago this was when I say I had stopped the analysis before I started the training.

Shortly before the end of the analysis, I dreamt that I was walking alone when I came to a gate. I looked over and saw a large coiled serpent asleep on the other side. At this point I took out a camera and leant over the gate to take photographs of the serpent. I was aware of feeling uneasy as I recounted this dream to my analyst, who looked concerned as she listened. She interpreted the dream to mean that I was behaving like a tourist in the unconscious and warned me of the dangers of awakening the sleeping serpent.

I paid little heed in spite of the inner voice of the self urging caution. The self 'knows' but, at the start of the individuating process, the ego has to behave in an heroic way and go forth on its adventure in spite of the perils ahead. Needless to say, the sleeping serpent did awake not long after and I then found myself caught in an incomprehensible state of confusion and panic attacks. This eventually forced me to return to analysis – this time with a different analyst. The dream marked the rite of passage that led eventually to my training as an analyst.

In explicating the images to be found in 'big' dreams, Jung writes the following:

> Here we find the dangerous adventures and ordeals such as occur in initiations. We meet dragons, helpful animals, and demons; also the Wise Old Man . . . the transformative processes and substances of alchemy . . . all things which in no way touch the banalities of everyday . . . they have to do with the realization of a part of the personality which has not yet come into existence but is still in the process of becoming. (Jung, 1960b: 293)

4

Criticisms and Rebuttals

As with the previous chapters, only some of the material that exists will be used to demonstrate the kind of criticisms that Jung, along with every seminal thinker, has been on the receiving end of since he first started to develop his own ideas. Some have already been touched on above, for instance, the statements declaring that he was overstepping the boundary of psychology into the territory of theology. There is a much greater exploration of this in the section on Martin Buber in this chapter, which will start with an exposition of the controversial issue of Jung's alleged pro-Nazi and anti-Semitic views.

Nazism and Anti-Semitism

The Göring Institute
In exploring the accusations against Jung in this area, it is necessary first to set the background to how psychotherapy and psycho-analysis came into being in Germany and, for this purpose, I have consulted the writings of the American student of German history and psychoanalysis, Geoffrey Cocks. He has steeped himself in the study of what happened in the dynamic field of medical psychology in Germany both before and after the advent of Hitler.

Briefly, psychoanalysis began to have an impact in Germany early in the century and its concepts challenged those of the psychiatric establishment which were grounded in mechanistic empiricism and heredity. Freud's achievement was to combine the preoccupation with the hidden forces in the psyche of the Romantics with that of nineteenth-century materialism. The German Psychoanalytic Society was founded in 1910. However, Freud's concern that it would remain labelled as the 'Jewish science' (see Chapter 1) was above all true in Germany under the Nazis when it was completely banned.

On the other hand, the history of psychotherapy in Germany took a different course. Due to the economic and political chaos resulting from the First World War and the fact that it was criticized by the medical establishment for being non-scientific, psychotherapy was not accepted until the late 1920s. The annual meeting of psychiatrists and neurologists in 1925 led to the first General Medical Congress for Psychotherapy in Baden-Baden followed in 1928 by the founding of the International General Medical Society for Psychotherapy. In 1930 a journal called the *Zentralblatt* came into being which covered matters to do with psychotherapy along with psychological medicine and hygiene. 'The primary purpose of the society and its annual congresses from 1926 to 1931 was to minimize the dissension among the various theories of psychotherapy . . . and to encourage research in the young field' (Cocks, 1997: 24).

In 1934 Jung became the President of the International General Medical Society for Psychotherapy, which was composed of rival factions such as the Adlerians, including Alfred Adler; Jungians, including Jung; Stekelians, including Stekel; and Freudians, including Karen Horney and Wilhelm Reich but not Freud; and a large number of eclectic psychotherapists. Jung, for his part, hoped that in making it internationally known, psychotherapy would be protected from extinction in Germany and he stated that he was planning an institute in Zurich based 'after our Berlin model' (Cocks, 1997: 133). Jung's stated intention in being associated with the Society was to act in the interest of its Jewish members. '. . . The Germans' use of Jung was also in his interest in promoting analytical psychology, particularly at the expense of its arch rival, Freudian psychoanalysis' (Cocks, 1997: 135). Cocks has no doubt that there was a genuine anxiety on Jung's part for the Jewish members of the society.

The membership of the Society as a whole comprised a largely Protestant and conservative constituency and it was this number who easily transformed themselves into supporters of the Nazi party after 1933 when Hitler became Chancellor of Germany. The medical profession in Germany held largely anti-Semitic views based on Social Darwinist theories of the survival of the fittest and eugenics. After 1918 at a time of economic hardship there was particular envy with regard to the successful Jewish physicians practising in Berlin and other large cities. Jacob Burckhardt, the well-known historian, expressed concern about the decline of civilization and attributed this to venal Jews. Jung never voiced such thoughts directly but was also concerned about the decline of spiritual values and hoped that the fascist movements of the 1920s and 1930s might provide an antidote.

The advent of Hitler as the Chancellor was followed by increasing persecution of the Jews, for instance, the expulsion of the predominantly Jewish psychoanalytic movement from that country.

Those members of the psychoanalytic movement who did not manage to escape were tortured and murdered in Nazi concentration camps.

What replaced it was a psychotherapy in service of the state which 'for the Nazis . . . existed as an extension of what they regarded as nature, ensuring the well-being of its inhabitants for the purpose of cultivating their potential for its use . . . Health policy . . . was not so much a matter of care of the sick but of care of the healthy' (Cocks, 1997: 92). For this reason, the psychotherapist's role in the Nazi regime was to be an active agent on behalf of the community in leading patients to live healthy and productive lives.

According to Cocks, the founders of German psychotherapy were keen to have Jung associated with it in order to provide the prestige associated with his reputation. For Jung's part, Cocks has no doubt that the former was motivated by genuine anxieties about the survival of psychotherapy in Germany under the Nazis but he also claims that Jung and the other German psychotherapists were enthusiastic about National Socialism. As was shown in the preceding chapters, the kind of psychology that Jung was developing was strongly influenced by mythological motifs linked to a teleological orientation. The philosophy underlying this approach appeared to be in line with Nazi ideology. 'More than one Nazi racial theoretician saw Jung's work as indispensable in providing rich material for the history and culture of a race' (Cocks, 1997: 137).

In a broadcast in 1933 in an interview over Radio Berlin, Jung said 'every movement culminates organically in a leader' (Cocks, 1997: 139). He declared that there was a different European soul to the German one which was 'youthful' and that Europe could not understand Germany because it did not share the same heritage and psychological experiences. Jung even went on to approve Hitler's assertion that the individual must go his own way without taking issue with the totalitarian attitudes of the Nazi regime.

Jung's actions between 1933 and 1940 have caused a great deal of controversy and Cocks's research reveals a complicated situation with regard to Jung during these years. Enthusiasm for Jung in Germany did not mean that analytical psychology had carte blanche there. For instance, in 1936 participation by Germans was not allowed at the annual Jungian Eranos Conference at Ascona in Switzerland because Jews attended in large numbers and because some of the topics were 'politically conflictual'. However, it has to be said that most of Jung's protests about the course of events in Germany were only seen or heard by non-Germans and were not voiced in the country itself.

Although Jung was President of the International General Medical Society until 1940 when he finally resigned, he did not take an active part in its internal workings but confined himself to the international congresses organized under its aegis. His role in German psychotherapy diminished considerably after the founding of the Göring Institute in 1936 but it is in his role as editor of the *Zentralblatt* that he provoked most criticism. In this capacity: 'Genuinely independent and perceptive people have for a long time recognized that the difference between Germanic and Jewish psychology should no longer be effaced, something that can only be beneficial to the science' (Cocks, 1997: 140). This distinction between Jewish and German science was attacked by many people outside Germany as it was a theme put forward by German intellectuals in support of the Nazi regime.

The same issue of the *Zentralblatt* contained an article by Matthias Göring which was full of pro-Nazi rhetoric so that Jung's remarks could be used by German colleagues to associate his name and theory as sanctioning the Nazi regime. This was all the more the case as the journal was published in Germany. 'Regardless of their context, however, Jung's observations were objectionable in and of themselves to many, as they seemed to support the official anti-Semitism of the Nazi government' (Cocks, 1997: 140).

Jung again wrote an article for the journal in 1944 seeking to distinguish between an 'Aryan' and a Jewish unconscious claiming that Freud 'did not know the German soul, and neither do any of his blind adherents. Has not the shattering advent of National Socialism, upon which the world gazes with astonished eyes, taught them better?' (Cocks, 1997: 141). Jung's criticism was addressed at Freud's materialism and the rootlessness of modern Jewish culture and of the anti-Christian orientation of the psychoanalysts. In a letter to a colleague he stated: '. . . in this instance the Aryan people can point out with Freud and Adler, specific Jewish points of view are publicly preached and, as can likewise be proved, points of view that have an essentially corrosive character' (Cocks, 1997: 142).

Cocks holds a middle position between pointing to Jung's lack of judgement in making the above statements and damning him as a Nazi collaborator. He acknowledges that Jung's cultural relativism never deteriorated from differentiating to denigrating Jews in the crude and vicious way that the Nazis did and goes on to say:

> While Jung's words here betrayed some ethically dubious habits of mind, Jung's opponents have often reduced these pronouncements to proof of unalloyed anti-Semitism and wholehearted collaboration with the Nazis.

Such a view, however, ignores Jung's increasing disaffection toward the Nazis and his desire to protect psychotherapists in Germany. (Cocks, 1997: 146)

At the same time as taking Jung's critics to task, Cocks also observes that his defenders must be more candid about 'the disturbing ambiguities in his thought, especially with regard to Jews' (Cocks, 1997: 146). He asserts that uncritical admirers of Jung have tried to render harmless the latter's assertions at a politically sensitive time. The most common approach amongst the first generation of Jungians after the Second World War was to deny that he was anti-Semitic in any way. Another has been to ignore the problem completely. 'The third approach is to argue simplistically that Jung made mistakes rather than acting out of evil intent' (Cocks, 1997: 146).

By 1939 relations between Jung and Göring were worsening and there was no congress held that year. The latter was concerned by what he saw as Jung's anti-German views in various ways, one being the latter's attempts to get non-Germanic or axis powers to join the General Medical Society. Instead Göring asserted that 'it would be very good if the authoritarian states were to join the international society so that the liberalistic states would not maintain superiority' (Cocks, 1997: 144).

By this time, Jung was clearly more jaundiced in his view of the Nazis as in the following:

> The impressive thing about the German phenomenon is that one man, who is obviously 'possessed', has infected a whole nation to such an extent that everything is set in motion and has started rolling on its course to perdition. (Cocks, 1997: 142)

In 1938 after the Night of Broken Glass and the attacks on the Jewish community, the C.G. Jung Society along with others lost its official status as a registered association. Cocks summarizes Jung's stance towards Nazism as a dialectic between prejudice and tolerance in which the latter eventually won out. However, he disagrees with the Jungian, Wolfgang Giegerich's point that Jung was

> purposefully engaging the shadow of racial prejudice in order to extirpate it. Such a judgment naively ignores the plurality of motives and conditions present in any human action . . . (and) turns a blind eye to the negative effects of Jung's lack of early criticism of Hitler and the possible legitimacy for the regime created in the minds of many or some through Jung's association with it. (Cocks, 1997: 150)

'Carl Gustav Jung and the Jews: The Real Story'

James Kirsch, in the above-titled paper published in 1982, explores the case against Jung and ends by declaring him completely exonerated. 'The fact that some of Jung's statements concerning Jews are problematic is not denied . . . and his later rejection of his former views should be considered as the overriding feature in judging Jung' (Kirsch, 1982: 113). Kirsch had taken issue with Jung after the Second World War about some of these views but, in the end, declared himself satisfied that Jung was not anti-Semitic.

Kirsch's own background is that he studied with Jung in 1929 and remained in frequent contact with him until the latter's death in 1961. He went on to become a Jungian analyst and founded the Society of Jungian Analysts of Southern California.

He has quotes from Jung which show him in a moral conflict about whether to remain neutral and within the Swiss frontier or to venture into Germany and bring on himself what he calls the inevitable misunderstandings of anyone who had dealings with the political powers there. According to his Secretary, Aniela Jaffé, in the article she wrote entitled 'Jung and National Socialism', Jung accepted the post of president of the General Medical Society at the urgent request of its leading members and managed to redraft the statutes so that Jewish psychotherapists could become members. At the same time his assistant, C.A. Meier, became the Secretary-General of the Society and the managing editor of the *Zentralblatt*. According to Jaffé, Jung and Meier did this in order to keep the young science of psychotherapy alive in Germany and to come to the aid of Jewish colleagues in Germany.

Jaffé also takes up the problematic of Jung's ambivalent attitude to Jews, quoting him as saying, on the one hand, '. . . the Jew, who is something of a nomad, has never yet created a cultural form of his own . . . since all his instincts and talents require a more or less civilized nation to act as a host for their development' (Kirsch, 1982: 122). On the other hand, he protested that he was no more trying to depreciate Semitic psychology when he talked of the 'personal equation' than 'it is a depreciation of the Chinese to speak of the peculiar psychology of the Oriental' (Kirsch, 1982: 122).

She does admit that he was willing to give National Socialism the benefit of the doubt in the early years: 'The "Aryan" unconscious contains creative tensions and "seeds of a future yet to be born" was the psychological foundation of his hopes' (Kirsch, 1982: 123).

Kirsch reports that in a conversation he had with Jung in Berlin in 1933, the latter had hopes that there might be a positive outcome to the Nazi movement. He could not accept Kirsch's completely pessimistic view and the latter's intention of leaving Germany as soon as possible. When Kirsch saw Jung in 1947, the latter remembered this conversation and apologized for it. Jung's view was based on his theory of *archetypes* which would see a mass movement as being essentially archetypal – containing both evil and good – and capable of producing diametrically opposite results.

For Jung, therefore, National Socialism was a manifestation of the storm-god, Wotan, that represented an outburst of the collective unconscious and he counted on the healing and creative forces in the human psyche to do their work. When this failed to happen with regard to the Nazi movement and the full extent of their horrors became known, Jung revised his hope and from then on was publicly critical of it.

Jaffé states that the psychic background to Jung's ambivalent feelings towards Jews has its deepest roots in the relationship between Freud and Jung:

> . . . it ended tragically in mutual resentment which has never quite died out . . . In their friendship and separation, so spotlighted by the world, it was not only two great personalities that confronted one another in scientific and man-to-man discussion, not only the old master and the young disciple, but, above all, the Jew and the gentile. (Jaffé, 1989: 96)

One of the criticisms of Jung's ambivalence towards the Nazis is that it stemmed from an unconscious power-drive but Kirsch completely dismisses this and says that Jung had integrated the collective unconscious to such a degree that he had acquired enormous power from that and had no need of an ego-power-drive.

Kirsch also points to the sensitivity to anti-Semitism of Jews and quotes Ernest Jones as follows:

> I became, of course, aware, somewhat to my astonishment, of how extraordinarily suspicious Jews could be of the faintest sign of anti-Semitism and of how many remarks of actions could be interpreted in that sense. The members most sensitive were Ferenczi and Sachs; Abraham and Rank were less so. Freud himself was pretty sensitive in this respect. (Jones, 1955: 163)

Kirsch acknowledges that although Jung tried to help Jews from the beginning of the time that the Nazis took over in Germany, he had an unresolved 'Jewish' complex. This had been activated in him by the relationship with Freud – at first in a positive way which transformed later into negative and critical feelings that extended to Jews in general. According to Kirsch, Jung completely liberated himself from it finally by writing *Answer to Job*.

New Research

Thomas Kirsch, the son of James Kirsch whose paper has been explored above, has conducted some original research into the issue of Jung's involvement with the Nazis during the 1930s in his book, *The Jungians: A Comparative and Historical Perspective*. Some of this research relates to Gustav Richard Heyer, who was the first significant person in Germany to be drawn to Jung's ideas. He and his wife had a short analysis with Jung in the mid-1920s and most German students of analytical psychology went to Heyer for analysis and training.

Heyer had National Socialist affiliations and claimed that it was Jung's own recommendation that he join the Nazi party. However, T. Kirsch cites a document housed in the National Library in Berlin, written by Heyer in February 1944, that states as follows:

> I did my training analysis with C.G. Jung in whose teachings the break-through was made from 'alien' construct. Yet today I cannot underwrite everything he published. Several things differentiate us, for instance, that he is more researcher than physician; that he does not value my inclusion of the feminine into psycho-therapy, and besides such scientific differences there are also different attitudes to political situations. (Kirsch, 2000: 126)

In 1945, Jung wrote to a colleague in Munich that he would have nothing further to do with Heyer because of the latter's Nazi affiliations. T. Kirsch also states that a number of Jewish people who saw Jung during the 1930s say that they detected no trace of anti-Semitism in him. T. Kirsch's mother, also an analyst, told him that it was through her analysis with Jung that she came to understand what it meant to be Jewish.

> Everyone looks for a 'smoking gun' to prove that Jung was really a Nazi way back when. It is not there. What Jung did not do is openly and publicly repudiate the Nazis before the war. That criticism could be made of many other influential people. There is still the expectation that Jung, as a depth psychologist, should have known better. (Kirsch, 2000: 132)

T. Kirsch raises the question as to whether Jung's theories promote racism, for instance, the hypothesis of the collective unconscious. For his own part, he does not believe them to have a racist bias and, in any case, they are open to scientific enquiry. He declares that he feels a sense of relief about the fact that personal anecdotes told to him by many Jewish people point to the fact that Jung pulled away from any association with the Nazis possibly as early as 1934.

Recently, T. Kirsch has had an exchange of letters with Harold Blum, the director of the Freud Archive in New York, in the new journal *Psychoanalysis and History*, in which Blum called Jung a Nazi. (Personal communication with Thomas Kirsch.)

Lingering Shadows

Maidenbaum and Martin's book, *Lingering Shadows*, published in 1991, grew out of a New York conference in 1989 and from papers given at a workshop during the Eleventh International Congress for Analytical Psychology in Paris in the same year. At both these, debates focused on the question of Jung's involvement with the Nazis and the related issues about whether he was anti-Semitic, self-promoting or just unfortunate in being where he was in the 1930s.

Contributors to the book itself were drawn from a wide source, including Jungians. This section already includes coverage from their own sources by some of the writers represented in *Lingering Shadows*, but one fascinating chapter deserves special mention and that is the one contributed by the psychoanalyst, Micha Neumann, son of a close colleague of Jung's, the analytical psychologist, Erich Neumann.

During the 1930s, Jung and Neumann corresponded on Jewish matters and the latter implored Jung to delve more deeply into these and tried to keep up his positive relationship with Jung. In the end, for E. Neumann, the inner connection to Jung was more important than their different human experiences as Jew and Christian and the unpleasantnesses that occurred between them. After *Kristallnacht*, E. Neumann wrote to Jung on 15 December 1938:

> I do not know if you can imagine how difficult it is to maintain an inner relationship with a man who naturally feels, at most, a superficial connection to the events that injure all of us Jews . . . Still I feel the need to write to you once again in order to sustain within me the feeling that even for a Jew like myself there still exists some piece of Europe. (Maidenbaum and Martin, 1991: 282)

Micha Neumann takes a different view to his father and says that there was a blind spot in Jung with regard to the Jews that had its roots in the complicated and conflict-laden relationship with Freud. This was due not only to the father projections onto Freud but also had strong elements of religious contents.

> He identified himself unconsciously with Nazi symbols, ideology, and anti-Semitism. He believed in the positive collective 'Germanic soul', to which he felt he belonged. Is it not true that Jung's shadow remained repressed and cut off from his own consciousness? (Maidenbaum and Martin, 1991: 276)

One telling incident recorded at the back of the book and told to this writer by Hella and Gerhard Adler, is that of Franz Riklin's visit to Vienna in 1938. A large sum of money was gathered together by some rich Swiss Jews and Riklin was sent with this to Austria in order to try to bring out some of the prominent Jews. He went to see Freud with this offer but the latter responded: 'I refuse to be beholden to my enemies.' Riklin knew that Jung would be very sorry but, although sad, Jung was not surprised saying: 'He (Freud) would not take help from me under any circumstances' (Maidenbaum and Martin, 1991: 382).

The Political Psyche

Andrew Samuels, another contributor to the above book, has been instrumental in opening up these issues within the Jungian community. In his book *The Political Psyche* Samuels says that both defenders and attackers of Jung are sitting in judgment on him and looking for a 'final solution' to the Jung problem. As Samuels expresses it: 'The shadows surrounding Jung are going to linger, for they want us to pay psychological attention to them' (Samuels, 1993: 294).

Samuels takes issue with those who defend Jung on the grounds that he was a man of his times, for instance, the Jungian Adolf Guggenbühl-Craig's statement that 'the anti-semitism of Jung was a sheer banality of the collective he belonged to' (Samuels, 1993: 294). In response, Samuels cites a number of criticisms of Jung in the 1930s, one being that of the philosopher and critic Walter Benjamin who studied Jung's works in order to criticize them on political grounds. In Benjamin's opinion Jung had 'leaped to the rescue of the Aryan soul with a therapy reserved for it alone' (Samuels, 1993: 295). A month later he wrote that Jung's psychology was 'the devil's work' (Samuels, 1993: 296).

Many of the articles that appeared in the *Zentralblatt* at the time of Jung's editorship consisted of repeated attacks on 'Jewish' mental states countered by praise for Aryan psychology. Many also praised Hitler and the Nazi party. Even though the journal was published in Germany and Jung and Meier were editing it from Zurich there were occasions when anti-Semitic statements were taken out by Jung or Meier or papers by Jewish writers included. Samuels asks why they only sometimes exercised their editors' discretion and what to make of the fact that many anti-Semitic ideas were allowed to be published in the journal.

Samuels has made a study of one of the co-signed pieces that Jung wrote for the journal with Matthias Göring – a 70th birthday tribute to Dr Robert Sommer in which they particularly praise a new chapter in a book he wrote in 1927. The following lines from that chapter are indicative of many others: 'There has been an intrusion of alien blood into the Germanic race'; 'The type of the Nordic race . . . forms a contrast . . . to the backwards sloping forehead of the primitive human races'; 'The selection of the gifted has to be performed' (Samuels, 1993: 299).

The reason Samuels puts forward for Jung's approval of these statements is echoed in Cocks above: that Jung's position at the head of German psychotherapy enabled him to promote analytical psychology. Freud had maintained that psychoanalysis had to be accepted in Germany before it came into its own. 'History, and Hitler, put that goal within Jung's grasp' (Samuels, 1993: 299).

The point Samuels is making is that Jung's papers and editorials in the 1930s related to racial and national psychologies, in particular the kind of disturbing statements he made about Jewish culture and psychology could easily be taken to be underwriting Nazi ideology. One instance of this is what Jung said about the Jews never having created a cultural form of their own but needing a 'host nation' in order to develop has strong echoes of Hitler's image of the Jews as parasitic.

If Jung had only been the president of the General Medical Society in support of his aim to save psychotherapy in Germany and to protect the rights of Jewish psychotherapists then there would be far less controversy over his activities still in evidence today. Samuels cites Jung's own theory of meaningful coincidences that is called *synchronicity*, to demonstrate the merging of Jung's thoughts with his actions: '. . . the psychic world (his ideas on Jewish psychology, perhaps) and the social world (German politics, perhaps) are acausally intertwined' (Samuels, 1993: 302).

Defenders of Jung claim that he was not personally anti-Semitic but even here Samuels produces evidence to the contrary. Michael Fordham has reported that on meeting Jung for the first time he was greeted with a long harangue against the Jews and the 'parasitic elements in Jewish psychology'.

Again in a letter Jung wrote in 1945 to Mary Mellon, the wife of the American multi-millionaire, Paul Mellon, he says:

> you probably have heard the absurd rumor that I am a Nazi. This rumor has been started by Freudian Jews in America . . . I found a falsified photo of mine in the Psychological Seminar of Calcutta University. It was a photo retouched in such a way as to make me appear as an ugly Jew . . . It is however difficult to mention the anti-christianism of the Jews after the horrible things that have happened in Germany. But Jews are not so damned innocent after all – the role played by the intellectual Jews in prewar Germany would be an interesting object of investigtation. (Samuels, 1993: 304)

Blood and Soil

Samuels points to the twin concepts in Jung's thinking that link it with National Socialist ideas around leadership and nation. These are discussed at length in *The Political Psyche*, and the interested reader is directed to that book for further reading.

This section will content itself with a brief look at Jung's own ambivalence about leadership which found expression, on the one hand, in his denial of leadership ambitions in trying to create a following in the much-quoted statement: 'Thank God I'm Jung and not a Jungian'. In contrast to this are his statements in the interview on Radio Berlin in 1933, alluded to above, where he appeared to accept the idea of a *Führer* – in other words of unquestioned leadership. Jung did display attributes of leadership in many of his statements, including his ideas around individuation, but there is still an atmosphere of denial about this in the Jungian community which prefers to see him instead as only unworldly.

The idea of nation that was common to both Jung and National Socialism was that of blood and soil. This postulates that the land in or on which an individual lives not only influences the psyche and the psychological development of that individual; it can, according to Jung, even cause profound physiological changes such as the size of the skull.

It was Jung's attempt to found a cultural psychology that brought him into line with Nazi thinking. Further, his fascination with the question of leadership added to the nexus between the two. Both have their roots in Germanic Romantic philosophy which, when activated, can result in powerful forces being unleashed in the psyche on a mass or individual level. In Zurich in 1946 Jung admitted to Rabbi Leo Baeck that he had 'slipped up'.

The Case of Dr Carl Gustav Jung

The section on Jung's activities in this area will close with an account from a file that came into my possession some time back. About 13 or 14 years ago, I was informed that there existed a file on Jung at the British Foreign Office accusing him of being a Nazi collaborator. This document is mentioned in several accounts by people who have never seen it often with a strong bias indicating that it provides proof of Jung's alleged pro-Nazi sympathies.

Attempts to get hold of this file had so far been unsuccessful so I contacted a friend in the Cabinet Office and asked if he could do anything to obtain it. The next thing I knew was that the file arrived by post with the compliments of the Foreign Office. It is entitled 'The Case of Dr. Carl Gustav Jung: Pseudo-scientist Nazi Auxiliary by Maurice Léon'.

The file was put together in 1946 at the time of the Nuremberg Trials (I am using the same spelling as the document). It contains a 15-page denunciation of Jung by a man living in New York called Maurice Léon. There is nothing in the file to show who he is or from where he originates and enquiries at the Foreign Office have been to no avail in this regard. As a result, there is a restriction on copyright to do with the document itself as permission cannot be sought. This means that I can only give a summary of the content of his denunciation of Jung and will not be able to include lengthy verbatim extracts from the document itself.

The file also includes a few letters from officials at the Foreign Office and the latter have generously granted permission for me to reproduce them. As they are quite short, I will quote them in full.

It is difficult to know how to appraise the Léon document as it is an uneasy mix of the horrors of the Nazi regime combined with slightly comical accounts of Jung's personal and professional life. The plaintiff starts by saying that the letters column of the *New York Herald Tribune* of 22 November 1945 contained correspondence for and against Jung as a Nazi. Léon himself is quite sure that Jung was and cites the latter's 'blatant outburst' in support of the over-running of Russia. He goes on to say that supporters of Nazism should be held responsible for the horrors of Dachau, Buchenwald and Auschwitz.

From there he proceeds to say that since Jung's deviation from Freud, his followers have been made up of frustrated women who claim that he is of ancient Swiss descent whereas Léon declares that he is German.

Visitors to Jung's house 'of rather forbidding mysterious exterior' in Kusnacht were received 'by Jung's wife, a woman of sad countenance who acted as an assistant to her husband, but in a capacity secondary to that of Jung's principal assistant, Fraulein Toni Wolff.' Jung himself is described as 'a tall, gray-haired man of enigmatic mien'. Patients and other visitors succeeded one another at hourly intervals and were charged 50 Swiss francs each. Wealthy Americans were amongst these, including an American Senator whom Jung apparently claimed to have cured but who died soon after. The American women who came were either accompanied by their husbands or not and in the latter case this often resulted in divorce.

The document goes on to assert that 'these two great minds (Hitler's and Jung's) concurred in favouring a specifically German religion' over the Ten Commandments and the Sermon on the Mount. It also gives an account of the General Medical Society and claims that Jung knew what the Nazis were doing in concentration camps.

Jung's article on Wotan is portrayed as a justification of Nazi neo-paganism in comparing it to what the Jews did to others in the name of Jehovah and the Moslems in the name of Allah – 'another Semitic experience of God'. Most of the rest of the document is based on this paper of Jung's and on the assertion that he, like the Nazis, was caught in the paganism that was unleashed at the time. Léon concludes that: 'Only those who pursue illusions will believe that the sadistic madness implanted in German minds will soon disappear. The process may take a century.' He advocates that Jung, as the leader of the intellectuals who supported the Nazis, should be brought to justice in Germany along with his confederate Hermann Göring.

This document was sent to Lord Vansittart, a well-known Germanophobe, who wrote on 6 March 1946 to a Mr P. Dean in the Legal Adviser's Department at the Foreign Office as follows:

Dear Mr Dean,
I am sending the enclosed to you because I was asked to do so by Maurice Léon, who is a good friend of ours and very influential in the United States. I don't suppose there is anything to be done about Jung as he seems to be Swiss now, but Dr. Göring is just the sort of fellow who ought to be brought to book, together with a great number of his fellows.
Yours sincerely, Vansittart

Pat Dean's assistant replied as follows on 25 March 1946:

Dear Lord Vansittart,
Many thanks for your letter of the 6th March addressed to Pat Dean enclosing two copies of an article by Maurice Léon.
We are sending a copy of the article to Dean who is now in the Control Commission in Berlin.
Yours sincerely, F.F. Garner

F.F. Garner wrote to Mr P. Dean at the British War Crimes Executive, Nuremberg, on 25 March 1946, as follows:

Dear Dean,
I enclose herewith a copy of an article by a Mr. Maurice Léon which was sent to us by Lord Vansittart under cover of a letter addressed to you. We feel that the best thing to do with this article is to put it straight into the waste paper basket and forget about it.
We are acknowledging receipt of Lord Vansittart's letter and are telling him that we have passed a copy of the article on to you.
Yours sincerely, F.F. Garner

Martin Buber's Criticism

The religious philosopher, Martin Buber, had positive relations with Jung from the early 1920s when Emma Jung had taken part in his week-long conference on Taoism in the Netherlands. Subsequently, Buber had read a few of Jung's essays, which he said had made a positive impression on him, and had taken part in the Jungian Eranos Conference at Ascona in 1934. In his book, *Religion and Modern Thinking*, Buber had called Jung the leading psychologist of the day in making religion comprehensible in its historical and biographical forms.

It was, therefore, a shock to many people in Europe, America and Israel when the controversy between Buber and Jung emerged in 1951 with the former's critique of the latter, accusing him of being a Gnostic and not a psychologist. This was shocking to many because the traditional enemy of religion was Freud, while Jung was seen as its great friend. Also, many of Jung's followers were close to Buber in sharing with both men a concern for modern man's search for a soul and the *collective unconscious* has a transpersonal and *numinous* (i.e. awe-inspiring) feel to it.

The real issue for Buber was that it is that part of Jung's thinking that transmutes faith into *gnosis* (knowledge) which amounts to a Gnostic transformation of faith that accounts far more than any other thinking for what Buber called the 'eclipse of God'. 'This same issue of *gnosis* – knowing *about* faith – versus *devotio* – *actually living faith* in the dialogue of addressing and being addressed' (Friedman, 1991: 356). For Buber, the real crisis of our time is the struggle between gnosis, which wants to know, and devotio, which wants to serve and sanctify. 'The difference between the world with God and without God is so enormous that the discussion of God must divide except in a group united by a real common faith' (Schaeder, 1973: 464).

In his book, *Eclipse of God*, Buber took issue with Jung and the German philosopher, Martin Heiddeger. Although he respected the service that Jung's psychological research had rendered to religious thinking, his criticism of Jung rested on his assertion that psychology must observe its limits and is not authorized to judge religion as an aspect of actual human existence. The 'eclipse of God' or suspension of the ethical in our age means that 'honest men lie and compassionate men torture'. This eclipse was above all due to the Holocaust, which violated existential trust in a way that nothing had before. 'When God seems to withdraw himself utterly from the earth and no longer participates in its existence' (Friedman, 1986: 148).

With each new crisis the contract between the universe and humans and the community and humanity is dissolved and human beings find themselves solitary and homeless in the world. 'The question about man's being faces us as never before in all its grandeur and terror – no longer in philosophical attire but in the nakedness of existence' (Friedman, 1986: 151).

Buber saw Jung as a modern Gnostic and thought that this was more dangerous to the 'eclipse of God' than Heidegger's writing on 'being'. The following statement by Buber makes this clear:

> The psychological doctrine which deals with mysteries without knowing the attitude of faith towards mystery is the modern manifestation of gnosis. Gnosis is not to be understood as only a historical category, but as a universal one. It – and not atheism, which annihilates God because it must reject the hitherto existing images of God – is the real antagonist of the reality of faith. Its modern manifestation concerns me specifically not only because of its massive pretensions, but also in particular because of its resumption of the Carporcratian motif. This motif, which reaches as psychotherapy, is that of mystically deifying the instincts instead of hallowing them in faith. (Friedman, 1991: 358)

The issue for Buber here is that truth is either reduced to the psychic and becomes mere tautology or the psychic is elevated to truth and becomes a false hypostasizing. This is because Jung is not a traditional Gnostic who believes in a transcendental God but a modern one who puts forward in its stead the collective unconscious and the self. Buber goes on to say that these can never be addressed as 'Thou' or engaged with in real dialogue as with the transcendent yet present Hebrew God. There is no sense of God needing humanity nor of God as the Creator – instead the divine is placed in the unconscious psyche and in this way becomes psychologized.

> If Jung had not asserted the psyche as *the* exclusive touchstone of reality, he could have bestowed great honour upon a realm that undoubtedly has profound meaning . . . without hypostasizing that realm into an inverted Platonic universal and elevating this larger-than-life-size sphere to the now empty throne of the Absolute. (Friedman, 1991: 359)

Buber's critique of Jung was closely related to his Hasidic teachings in which he says that what ancient Christian and non-Christian Gnostics and recent Gnostical movements have in common with psychoanalysis is the following. Those particular Gnostic movements reject all creation as evil and incapable of being hallowed but, the argument runs, the 'elect' being completely holy have the task of making everything unhallowed holy. In this way, they are encouraged to sin in order to raise sin to holiness by preserving an inner intention of purity in contrast to the deed.

This demonic 'lust for overrunning reality' to use Buber's words, amounts to a crisis in people's souls of temptation and dishonesty. He saw Jung's analytical psychology and psychoanalysis in general to be advocating an illusory belief that personal fulfilment can be found through the release of deep inner forces and that Jung's psychology, in particular, pointed to succumbing in part to evil as the road to the integration of the self and thus to individuation. This leads to the marriage of good and evil and the new incarnation where God is replaced by the deified or divine man.

Buber wrote to Jung: 'We are revealed to ourselves – and cannot express it otherwise than as something revealed' (Schaeder, 1973: 470). Further, that my 'self' is realized by taking the path 'at which, executing for my part the design which I am, I encounter the divine mystery of my created uniqueness, the mystery waiting for me' (Schaeder, 1973: 470).

In 1946, some years before he openly criticized Jung, Buber was already writing that in Jung and Karl Kerényi's introduction to a book on mythology, the latter was writing about myth as arising out of contact with the world; whereas Jung understood it as arising of its own in the soul.

The growing distance between the two thinkers affected some of Jung's followers and the most important of Jung's followers to defect to Martin Buber was Hans Trüb. The two met in 1923 at the Analytical Psychology Club of Zurich and Trüb was the first to introduce Buber's ideas into the relationship between therapist and patient. The former had trained with Jung and was a friend of his – so much so that Jung had recommended Emma Jung to him for analysis.

The relationship that developed between Buber and Trüb was mutually formative and, as a result, Buber wrote about schizophrenics and borderline states. Trüb, for his part, came to see Jungian psychology as a strange mix of scientific research, medical practice, and Gnostic quasi-religious philosophy. He later left the Jungian movement and became a follower of Buber. The greatest impact he had on Trüb, according to the latter, was not through his philosophy but through the personal relationship that grew between them.

Although Buber was a Jewish religious philosopher and was vitally concerned at the time of the Nazi uprising with the threat to Jewish people, he was also concerned about the threat it posed to Christianity. In 1934, when he attended the Jungian Eranos Conference at Anscona, he responded to vicious attacks on Christianity by a number of Nazis who were present by saying that although it was not usually his role to defend Christianity, he felt on that occasion that he must do so.

Jung's Reply to Martin Buber

In responding to the charge made against him by Buber that he is a Gnostic, Jung says that he has been called that as well as the opposite, an agnostic. He says he has also been accused of being a theist and an atheist, a mystic and a materialist. He asserts that these criticisms are made by metaphysicians, whose business it is to know about things in the Beyond. For his part, he denies that he has made statements in the same way about such things.

As we saw in the section above on the Gnostics, Jung studied them with enthusiasm because they were the first thinkers to concern themselves, in their own way, with the collective unconscious. For his part, Jung states that he is dealing with anthropomorphic ideas but not with actual gods and devils, although due to their autonomy, they can behave like psychic *daimons*. This is interpreted by the theologian as the devil's work and Jung admits that that is close to psychic truth.

Jung claims that far from being a theologian, he is a psychiatrist whose prime aim is to investigate the psyche empirically and interpret the results. He feels that as Buber has no psychiatric experience, he cannot understand what Jung means by the 'reality of the psyche' and the dialectical process of individuation. The ego has always been confronted with psychic powers that have been given sacred names and identified with metaphysical beings. Analysis of the unconscious has shown that these forces produce archetypal images which, for the analyst are not inspired by the divine inspiration of the Holy Ghost except for the individual who has the gift of faith. Jung says that for him these 'powers of the unconscious' are psychic facts and not metaphysical ones as he knows them experientially only through cognition.

These forces are autonomous aspects of the *objective psyche* and act as the counter-pole to the subjective ego. In this way, they may come to be designated as a 'Thou' – Buber's term for the divine. For Jung, these numinous, or awe-inspiring forces, manifest their darker aspects in reality as the holocaust and the invention of the atomic bomb; but they are also the other side that is expressed in beauty, goodness, wisdom and grace.

'The reality of the psyche' is his working hypothesis which he has supported through empirical findings. He claims that Buber has mistaken his (Jung's) empiricism for Gnosticism and challenges him to prove that the facts that he has described are only inventions. If Buber could do this, then Jung says that he would admit that he is indeed a Gnostic but, in that case, the former would have to dismiss all religious experience as self-deception.

Jung goes on to assert that it is Buber's inability to understand how an 'autonomous psychic content' like the God-image can erupt into ego consciousness as a living experience. But he states that it is not for him as an empirical scientist to determine how such a psychic content may be dependent on the existence of a metaphysical deity. Jung goes on to ask which metaphysical deity Buber is citing – is it the God of the orthodox Jew or of the Christian? This is an unfortunate lapse on Jung's part as Buber was, in fact, himself subjected to much criticism from orthodox Jewry for his views. Jung goes on to claim that he is convinced that Buber's relationship to a divine 'Thou' is to that of an autonomous psychic content, which is defined one way by Buber and another by the Pope.

Jung then addresses Buber's criticism that God cannot exist apart from man even though the former has asserted that everything said about God is a human and therefore a psychological statement. Jung goes on to challenge Buber to demonstrate where there is an image of God that has not been made by humans. This archetype has been implanted by God in human beings' psyches so that they may glimpse an image of the divine that originates in their own psychic substance. Unfortunately, theologians of different denominations have been seized by this archetype and are always at each other's throats declaring their God to be the only true one.

Jung says that he discovered the existence of this archetypal force as the result of human experience and that what satisfies him about it is that it is both human and 'other'. Like all archetypes, it possesses great power and that is why it is essential that there is a dialectic between the ego and the other realm of the unconscious. The contents of the objective psyche are related to metaphysical ideas such as are found in Gnostic writings. It is on this misconception that Buber has formulated his criticism of Jung.

Jung goes on to suggest that Buber visits a psychiatric asylum or studies the autobiographies of the mentally ill such as *Wisdom, Madness and Folly*, by John Custance, or the famous *Memoirs of My Nervous Illness*, by Schreber, that Freud analysed. In these Buber would see that metaphysical ideas are expressed which do not proceed from Gnostic hypotheses. Jung also says, in answer to Buber's assertion that he has contributed to the 'eclipse of God' that what he has, in fact, pointed to is the withdrawal of projection. In other words, Jung states that if he claims that all statements about God have their origin in the psyche that does not mean that he is denying God or attempting to put man in God's place.

> Faith is certainly a splendid thing if one has it, and knowledge by faith is perhaps more perfect than anything we can produce with our laboured and wheezing empiricism. (Jung, 1977: 668)

Jung goes on to say that Christian dogma is of a higher order than the 'wild' philosophizing of the Gnostics and the scientific endeavours of the psychologist.

> [They] are the outcome of our daily labours in the sloughs of ordinary human existence and human pain. They are essentially irrational, and the philosopher who criticizes them as though they were philosophical concepts tilts against windmills and gets into the greatest difficulties, as Buber does with the concept of the self. (Jung, 1977: 668)

Jung's rebuttal is scathing in its tone throughout and not least at the end where he throws down the gauntlet to Buber and all the other theologians who baulk 'at my odious psychology' and says that they are welcome to try to heal patients with the word of God. The psychologist, on the other hand, has to deal with the grim realities of human nature and start from facts which need interpretation.

Critique of Jung's Gnosticism

Chapter 2 explored Jung's interaction with Gnosticism through the work of Robert Segal. We will return to him now in order to highlight the profound difference between Jung's approach and that of the Gnostics.

It is easy to see why Jung felt that his approach had a great affinity with that of the Gnostics because their creation myths understood in his terms are to do with the development of the psyche. The godhead may be taken to symbolize the unconscious which prior to its emanations is a perfect whole and is hermaphroditic in the same way that alchemy portrays. It is the emergence of matter alongside the immaterial godhead which equates with the ego emerging out of the unconscious and the *divine spark* is the link to the godhead.

For Jung, the unconscious was creative and spontaneously produced the ego, although in both systems the key paradox is why the godhead/unconscious strives to produce matter/ego which it then consistently tries to undo. The spontaneity of the process of creation is accompanied by its opposite wherein the godhead/unconscious continually tries to reclaim its creation. As a result, the ego struggles to be independent of the unconscious and when it achieves this it repudiates its origins. To quote Marie-Louise von Franz, every human is made up of:

> a pre-conscious totality in which everything is already contained, including consciousness . . . (and) an active tendency towards building up a separate consciousness, which, then, sometimes, in a Luciferian gesture, turns back to the pre-conscious totality and says: 'I was not created by you, I made myself.' (Segal, 1992: 22)

According to Gnostic thinking, ignorance keeps humans enslaved to the material world while gnosis (knowledge) frees them from it.

Knowledge itself is liberating in that revelation of a higher order automatically liberates one from the lower one. That knowledge can only come from the godhead and the dependence of humanity on it is equivalent in psychological terms to the ego's dependence on the unconscious. Gnostic myths advocate total identification with divinity, which in the Jungian view would lead to a dangerous inflation where ego becomes identified with the self. At the very least this results in arrogance but can also lead to psychosis which, in turn, leads to the dissolution of the ego.

The Jungian goal of individuation is not the rejection of ego consciousness in favour of the unconscious but to arrive at a balanced position between the two. In Gnosticism, the revelation necessitates forsaking the material world altogether. This is the central difference between the two paths and for Jung returning to the unconscious always has the goal of raising it to consciousness. As he says:

> Man's worst sin is unconsciousness, but it is indulged in with the greatest piety even by those who should serve mankind as teachers and examples. When shall we stop taking man for granted in this barbarous manner and in all seriousness seek ways and means to exorcize him, to rescue him from possession and unconsciousness, and make this the most vital task of civilization. (Segal, 1992: 24)

For Jung, the return to the initial unconscious state is a quest undertaken to elevate it to consciousness, whereas for the Gnostics that was the end goal. Conversely, for the Gnostics the ultimate search is for the undoing of the link between divinity and matter, as the latter is always seen as evil. In the Jungian approach, this would be tantamount to a negative dissociation of the unconscious from ego consciousness. 'In sum, Jung's progressive ideal is at odds with the regressive one of Gnosticism' (Segal, 1992: 27).

Further, Jung associates the godhead with the unconscious and God and Christ with the self. The opening up of a dialectic along the ego/self axis is the aim of Jungian analysis, not the toppling of one by the other. In this way the ego becomes supplemented by the self. In his studies of Gnosticism, Jung overlooked the fact that the return of the divine spark to the godhead is the goal which has been demonstrated and is quite other to that of Jungian therapy.

The reason Jung misinterpreted Gnosticism was because he equated it with alchemy in thinking that the Gnostic process of liberating the immaterial sparks from matter were the equivalent of the alchemical process of extracting gold from base metals. On closer inspection one sees that the two processes are completely dissimilar as gold is produced out of metals whereas in the Gnostic system the sparks have fallen into, and are imprisoned in, matter and await release.

For Jung in *Answer to Job*, the godhead had to create the world in order to realize itself, so that creation is seen to be necessary and beneficial. It is the union of the two that is the ultimate in divinity. This is completely at odds with the Gnostic view that all creation is evil and that matter's rediscovery of the godhead is an end in itself. From the Jungian standpoint, the Gnostic goal leads to inflation and not to individuation.

Gender

Rethinking has also taken place in the area of gender and three or four of these revisions will be briefly explored in this section. Further reading on the subject will be mentioned in the literature given at the back of the book.

Jung and the Feminine

The starting point will be the American analytical psychologist, Beverley Zabriskie's chapter in Renos Papadopoulos's *Carl Gustav Jung: Critical Assessments*. Zabriskie stresses the importance of gender in understanding the universe in a wide variety of disciplines ranging across mythology, geography, philosophy, history and many others.

She claims that a fascination with the feminine existed in earlier agrarian times as witnessed by figurines from that time that attest to a veneration of the female body. Her hypothesis is that this was due to women being valued as co-equals in the work they could contribute to alongside men. Once territorial conquest became the dominant ethos, male qualities of aggression were emphasized and a split took place between the masculine, equated with civilization, and the feminine, with nature. 'The son culture separated from the ancient Great Mothers' (Zabriskie, 1992: 365). This meant that females became increasingly the supporters of others and lost their independent identity.

To digress from Zabriskie for a moment, this shift from the importance of the feminine to that of the masculine has resulted in the former being symbolically castrated by the latter. Depth psychologists have described this in various ways; for instance, Freud as 'penis envy'; Adler as the 'masculine protest' over 'feminine weakness'; and Lacan as the 'symbolic order' which is associated with the phallic stage.

Jung's contribution to this was to equate consciousness and logos with the masculine and unconsciousness and eros with the feminine.

She applauds Jung's model of the *animus*, the archetype denoting the masculine principle, and *anima*, the feminine principle, and says that these enable the development of a balanced personality containing contrasexual elements. (New thinking has resulted in the revised concept of the yoked anima/animus seen to be part of every individual's inner world.)

According to Zabriskie, these creative ideas of Jung's became reified when they entered analytical psychology and 'became static. It is as if the archetypes fell into matter and reemerged as stereotypes' (Zabriskie, 1992: 365). Her balanced pronouncement on Jung's contribution to gender issues is that it has been both innovating as well as limiting, even damaging.

Jung and the Masculine

John Beebe's paper in the same book edited by Papadopoulos is on Jung's attitude to the masculine. This started to become a focus for male analytical psychologists in the late 1980s, including Andrew Samuels, Peter Tatham and James Wyly.

Beebe examines Jung's childhood dream of the phallic eye (which is reproduced at length in Chapter 1 of this book). He concludes that in his early thinking, Jung associated masculinity with consciousness, thus excluding the feminine dimension. Only later, when developing the archetype of the hero and initiation, did Jung come to a more mature view of masculinity. In particular, the myth of initiation involves 'the painful submission of the hero to the greater authority of archetypal forces with the power to mediate the development of consciousness' (Beebe, 1992: 363). This is the giving up of the consciousness associated with the hero and its arrogant nature.

This is an important insight into the paradox of the heroic stage which is, on the one hand, vital for leading the individual out of unconsciousness but must also be transcended for a further development of personality to take place. For a man, this must be accompanied by relationship to his anima that can enable him to relate to his masculine nature with 'the right emotional attitude' (Beebe, 1992: 364).

Beebe also sees Jung's earlier model of the Logos/Eros, discrimination/relatedness principles as inevitably leading to sexist rigidity, whereas the later, more mature formulation of the alchemical Sol and Luna which he developed when he was over 60 years old was 'grounded in the experience of masculine individuation after midlife' (1992: 365). This turning point led to the transformation of a rather naïve image of anima as full of potential. It has, instead, now gone through the suffering of tears and bitterness and is capable of ruthlessness when necessary. 'Luna is an initiated unconscious that is ready to interact with the initiated heroic consciousness that is Sol to produce the integration of personality' (Beebe, 1992: 364).

Alterity

Polly Young-Eisendrath states that Jung's theory of contrasexuality 'was cursed or blessed . . . with the Latin names of *anima* (for male contrasexuality) and *animus* (for the female counterpart)' (Casement, 1998: 202) Jung described these as archetypes and not complexes (Young-Eisendrath posits them as being the other way around) and saw them as biological consequences of the archetypal feminine and masculine. He went on to categorize them as universally accepted expressions of difference between the sexes.

Like Zabriskie, Young-Eisendrath criticizes the reifying of these terms into essentialist theorizing that led to sexual stereotyping and a formula based on complementarity. In this way, anima was split into an idealized feminine in being inspiring and life-giving or denigrated as negative hysteria and moodiness. A man could be talked of in this way as being in relationship to his anima or being in the grip of it.

Animus, on the whole, comes across as mostly negative in Jung's writings. It was Emma Jung who put forward a more positive view of it in describing it as a woman's logos.

In reducing Otherness, or *alterity* – the term used by Lacan – to a formula of complementarity, Young-Eisendrath condemns it as destructive of interest in and curiosity about one's own contrasexuality, which can open up unknown aspects of personality.

Anne Springer has also taken issue with Jung's anima/animus model, suggesting that these are too comprehensive and define fundamental reciprocal bipolarity as normative. Sex and gender are mixed in an unspecified way (Young-Eisendrath's criticism, too) and an inner and outer heterosexual couple becomes the ideal.

Springer proposes that anima/animus are abandoned as constructs either as complexes or as archetypes and, in their place, advocates the following: 'At most we should consider a striving for comprehensive emotional, affective, sexual and spiritual intimacy and encounter as archetypal' (Casement, 1998: 195).

Michael Fordham

Two of the major rebuttals of classical Jungian ideas came from Jungian analysts themselves: Michael Fordham and James Hillman, both of whom stamped their own vision on analytical psychology. Fordham linked it to psychoanalytic, initially Kleinian ideas, which was the beginning of a fertile integration of psychoanalytic theory and practice with analytical psychology. This is reflected today in the way many Jungian analysts work around the world. At first, this approach was confined chiefly to the UK where it led to a split in the Society of Analytical Psychology (SAP) and the more 'classical' practitioners, who remained loyal to their vision of Jung, left. There have been several splits in the Jungian movement usually along what may thought of as a clinical versus mythological divide. Other factors, including cultural ones, play a prominent part in these splits in different parts of the world – not least the clash of different personalities.

Hillman was equally revolutionary – though in a very different way – in his revision, which has come to be called Archetypal Psychology. This will be elaborated further in the section below, which is devoted to Hillman's ideas.

Fordham was amongst the most creative analytical psychologists and one of the few to formulate his own approach to Jungian psychology. He was also the acknowledged leader of the Jungian movement in the UK. In 1933, he was introduced to analytical psychology by H.G. Baynes, a leading early British Jungian. Fordham was one of the few leading analysts of his generation who was not analysed by Jung and this may have had a lasting effect on him as he always appeared to be something of an outsider. On the other hand, they did have a long personal as well as professional relationship and it was Jung himself who selected Fordham to be the editor of the *Collected Works*.

Fordham thought that Jung's work was complementary to and not in opposition to Freud's and he began to steep himself in psychoanalytical ideas. He was particularly drawn to those of Melanie Klein, and his pioneering work was to integrate analytical psychology with psychoanalysis in a way which has since been fruitful for many Jungians.

This section on Fordham will give one example of his theory and one of technique. Reference will be made to James Astor's *Michael Fordham: Innovations in Analytical Psychology*, as all of his main ideas are thoughtfully put together in that book. According to Astor, Jung was the inspiration behind all Fordham's work and the latter also had a great respect for Mrs Jung of whom he said: 'She very much had a mind of her own which was appreciative of but not subservient to that of her husband' (Astor, 1995: 33). He was the first Jungian to interest himself in the child's internal world and began to seek for origins of the self and individuating in childhood.

Primary Self
From this vast store of experience Fordham built up from working with infants and children, he came to infer that the child's ego developed out of the self. This led him to postulate that there was a *primary self* from which the ego emerged through contact with the environment. This meant that there was a self before there could be an ego. This is quite other to Jung's thinking, which described the self and the ego as centres of integration within the individual but saw the self as coming into greater prominence in the second half of life after the mid-30s.

According to Fordham, the primary self was an integrated whole but had a potential energy which in time contributed to ego development. The mechanism that drives this he called *deintegration* and *reintegration* and the parts of the self that deintegrated he termed *deintegrates* and these would retain aspects of wholeness. Examples of these are the hungry baby's cry which contributes to its biological adaptation, or to the kind of imagery creation that contains potential symbolic meaning. In the former it is an objective manifestation and in the latter a subjective one. This theory is both a structural as well as a dynamic one.

Fordham also moved away from notions of 'the self' to examining what he saw as part selves each felt equally to be 'myself'.

Syntonic Transference/Countertransference
Fordham began his writings on transference in 1957, bringing in the kind of clinical phenomena that were missing from the Jungian literature up to that time. He differentiated between two kinds of transference – the dependent in which 'repressed infantile contents are released' (Astor, 1995: 104). When these have been attended to then 'emergence of the self and its realization in consciousness' can occur through analysis of the archetypal transference.

He also discovered two kinds of countertransference: syntonic and illusory. The first describes the analyst's experience of parts of the patient being projected into him, which can provide him with valuable information about the patient's inner world. This necessitates the analyst being able to deintegrate so that parts of the analyst can spontaneously respond to the patient's need. As these parts are manifestations of the self, Fordham extrapolated from these experiences with patients what Jung meant when he talked about analysis as a dialectical procedure:

> based on processes which neither I nor my patient can control consciously, and that analysis depends on the relatively greater experience of the analyst in *deintegrating* so as to meet the patient's *disintegration*. (Astor, 1995: 113)

Countertransference Illusion

This applies to reactions aroused in the analyst by something that is taking place in the interaction with the patient that are to do with unresolved aspects of the former. Fordham cites a session with an 11-year-old boy in which he became aggressive towards the boy. As Fordham says, at that time in the session he ceased to be an analyst but was caught instead in an enactment. He realized as he allowed himself to get in touch with his own feelings that the interaction had briefly thrown him back to the time when he was a young boy with his mother.

Cambray cites an instance of Jung exhibiting illusory countertransference defensiveness:

> A memorable example of this is his countertransferentially laden handling of the 'normal' doctor whose dream of discovering an idiot child smearing itself with feces alone in the middle of a large room, cause Jung to find a pretext to precipitously end the analysis and to provide an explanation of the dream 'as something quite innocuous', and gloss over all the perilous details. (Cambray, 2000: 18)

Fordham's work gave a practical application to many of Jung's statements in relation to aspects of analytical theory, for instance the idea that the analyst is in the analysis, the self-regulating tendencies of the psyche, and the need to create a new theory for each patient. He also added vital new insights from psychoanalytic theory, particularly to do with the central importance of *projective identification* in the analytic work.

James Hillman

This section on James Hillman, an original thinker and poetic writer, will draw on two people's work, as follows: Leon Schlamm, Lecturer in Religious Studies at the University of Canterbury in Kent, and David Tacey, Head of Psychoanalytic Studies at La Trobe University in Melbourne, Australia.

Schlamm's lecture paper, 'James Hillman's School of Archetypal Psychology and Polytheistic Theology – Psychology and Religion', states that Hillman's Archetypal Psychology is the only really important attempt to present a post-Jungian interpretation of the inner life of human beings. Hillman is an original thinker and a poetic writer but both Schlamm and Tacey agree that Hillman is also a controversial figure – the former calling him a 'black sheep' in the Jungian community. Nevertheless, his work can only be understood in relation to Jung and his followers.

Hillman shares in common with Nietzsche an antipathy towards monotheism and Christianity in particular and claims, instead, that the psyche is polytheistic. 'According to Hillman, God is dead, but, he proposes, like Nietzsche, that the gods are alive' (Schlamm, unpublished). For Hillman, Freud and Jung are monotheistic and the former established the ego as master in the psychic house. Jung, for all his talk of the collective unconscious and archetypes, is ultimately concerned with unifying them all under the power of the self.

Consequently, Hillman rejects the path of individuation, which he sees as the heroic path of privileging one aspect of psyche over others. For Hillman, there is no salvation in individuation and he advocates, instead, the path of disintegration and pathology and of psychological pluralism. Taking up Jung's famous dictum that the 'gods have become diseases', Hillman advocates a remythologizing of analytical thinking. 'The necessity of pathologizing derives from the gods who show patterns of psychopathology' (Schlamm, unpublished). The gods have been repressed and return as our *complexes* so that there is no cure for pathology but a need to re-evaluate it as divine.

Schlamm illustrates the nexus between pathology and the divine by pointing to what Hillman has to say about hysteria – the starting point of psychoanalysis. For Hillman, the way in which the archetypal energy associated with Dionysus manifests in a distorted fashion as hysteria is because it has been repressed. In this way it manifests as the return of the repressed. Hysteria is generally associated with women just as the cult of Dionysus was – and it was hysteria in young women that initially led to the discovery of the unconscious.

As the gods express themselves through images and fantasies, there is an emphasis on both of these in Archetypal Psychology. Also central to the latter is the idea of 'soul-making' by which Hillman means that through a process of deepening the images of the soul, the images of the gods may be experienced. This is why he stresses the power of the image itself over the search for a meaning behind the image. Jung placed tremendous value on imagery but was also a Kantian in distinguishing the phenomena of archetypal images from that which lies behind them – 'the thing in itself'. In this way, the concept of archetype becomes reified and, for this reason, Hillman prefers the term archetypal.

Further, for Hillman, 'living one's myth' does not mean living one myth but, rather, living myth as at any one time each individual is enacting many myths. The interested reader is directed to Hillman's writings in *The Myth of Analysis*, *Revisioning Psychology* and *Archetypal Psychology*.

In 'Twisting and Turning with James Hillman', David Tacey argues that Hillman's work is primarily governed by two archetypal styles: 'a "Hermes" pattern that insists on fluidity, openness and complexity, and an "anima" emotionality that produces high-flown rhetoric, extremism and dramatic reversals' (Casement, 1998: 215). His declared mission is 'soul-making' – a legacy from Neo-platonic ways of thinking.

Tacey goes on to say that there is a tendency (with notable exceptions like the New York analyst Paul Kugler) in the Jungian world to ignore Hillman and to carry on as if his challenge to basic Jungian assumptions does not exist.

> Is this because Hillman destroys the Jungian ghetto that other Jungians want to cherish? Or perhaps the silence derives from envy, spite or contempt for the man who has constructed himself as the *enfant terrible* of the post-Jungian world? (Casement, 1998: 218)

Hillman, for his part, has responded by declaring that 'Jungians are not interested in ideas' and are 'second-rate people with third-rate minds' (Casement, 1998: 218). The main thrust of Hillman's critique of Jung himself stems from the former's claim that 'For Jung psyche is inside, whereas for our post-Jungian archetypal school, psyche is more out there in the world' (Casement, 1998: 225). By this he means that archetypal psychologists are not interested in being shut up inside the head or shut out from the world.

Tacey takes issue with him over this misrepresentation of Jung, as the latter, long before Hillman, was resistant to the idea of encapsulating psyche or soul within the human subject. Tacey suggests that Jung was postulating a kind of postmodern animism in his exploration of objective psychic experience which 'reveals itself as a cosmos in its own right' (Casement, 1998: 225). Also, Jung's ideas on synchronicity, the acausal relating of human subjectivity and world events posits a continuum between inner and outer reality.

An important area for both Jung and Hillman lies in their valuing of dream material but Hillman's perspective is very different, eschewing as it does classical Jungian concepts about dreams as 'compensatory'. Instead, he suggests that dreams emerge from an archetypal underworld which is completely other to the waking dayworld. He is not seeking to interpret dreams to add to an increase in consciousness but sees dreams as having a purpose of their own. As stated above, the focus in archetypal psychology is on imagery and the image itself.

In 1993, Hillman launched an attack on psychotherapy in general with *We've Had a Hundred Years of Psychotherapy and the World's Getting Worse*, in which he uses as the basis of his argument his claim that the modern age discovers the soul of the world through pathology and illness. This is, in fact, very close to Jung's view that the gods have become diseases and that the deepest forces in the human psyche are manifested in neuroses and illness. Hillman's pessimistic conclusion at the end of that book is: 'By removing the soul from the world and not recognizing that the soul is also in the world, psychotherapy can't do its job any more' (Casement, 1998: 224).

Miscellaneous

The last part of this chapter will pick up on a few often-voiced criticisms of classical Jungian psychology.

Jung proposed what he called the synthetic or prospective (promethean) approach as his way of conducting analysis which he opposed to what he denigrated as the reductive backward (epimethean) approach. A counter-argument sometimes put forward is to accuse classical Jungians themselves of being reductive – albeit in a different way, viz. that of reducing patient's material to archetypes. Michael Fordham reported that Emma Jung remarked to Jung: 'You know very well you are not interested in anybody unless they exhibit archetypes!' (Astor, 1995: 50). In any case, the concept of transcendence should apply to the promethean/epimethean opposition as it does to all opposites.

Another criticism has to do with the obfuscation on the part of some Jungian practitioners in relation to Jung's typology (described in detail in Chapter 3). The terms themselves are easily susceptible to misinterpretation and, in particular, all kinds of fictions congregate around the *feeling* function. The latter, along with the *thinking* function, is a way of evaluating so that something is seen as being 'good' or 'bad', 'nice' or 'nasty', 'beautiful' or 'ugly'. An individual whose bias is to a more thinking way of functioning will evaluate something, say an idea, as 'interesting' or 'uninteresting'.

The reason for particular confusion around the jargon-term 'feeling' is that the word 'feeling' has so many different connotations in English. For instance, 'feeling' in Jung's sense of the term is often confused with being in touch with feelings – something that usually only comes about after the sort of epiphany that can occur from time to time in the course of an in-depth analysis. Alternatively, there may be an 'Aha!' moment in the course of living when something commonplace is suddenly experienced in a different way.

'Feeling' is also often confused with emotion: a brief definition of the two is that feeling, in this sense of the word, is a subjective state that is internal and hidden from others that can extend over time (e.g. happiness, sadness and fear). 'Emotion' is an expression outside the organism which is time-limited and whose physiological correlates are changes in the heart-rate, the functioning of the viscera and the muscular system.

The confusion around the feeling function extends to half-baked assertions along the lines that someone is *only* a 'thinking' or a 'feeling' type. How any actual human being could perform the remarkable feat of being able to evaluate in a purely thinking way without any feeling entering into the equation or vice versa is reminiscent of Portia's dictum to Shylock that he may have his pound of flesh but without shedding a drop of blood. What appears as polarized in Jung's early theory of *Logos* and *Eros* gave way later to a transcendence of opposites with his concept of the *androgyne*.

Critique of Dream Analysis

Another Jungian analyst, and a close colleague of Fordham, Kenneth Lambert, criticized the classical Jungian approach to dream analysis. He identifies four areas that are problematic. One is to do with the fact that eliciting dreams from a patient can damage the spontaneous flow of material from the patient's unconscious. Secondly, the analyst ends up being nothing more than an interpreter if the whole process becomes reduced to an abstract analysis of dreams. Thirdly, the introduction of dream material into the process may be a transference/countertransference *enactment* – i.e. dreams being produced out of compliance or conversely the withholding of dreams. Lastly, insufficient attention is paid in the classical approach to psychic mechanisms in dreams like projection or introjection. It is vital to bear in mind that it is the patient that needs to be analysed *not* the dream. (See what is said about dream analysis in Chapter 3.)

Psychic Reality

A trenchant criticism, echoing Hillman, comes from Marilyn Nagy, who says that Jung's subjectivist argument for the validity of psychic contents (*psychic reality*) has brought positive but also unhappy results. She particularly applies this to the training institutes where critical thinking has been squashed in favour of 'creating a kind of confessionalist atmosphere' (Nagy, 1991: 32). The doctrinal position that is fostered by this militates against open enquiry and hard thinking: 'a neglect of comparative research and the work of careful thinkers in related fields will eventually cost Jung's followers the very trust which their emphasis on the experience of the individual seeks to earn' (Nagy, 1991: 32).

An exciting conference on Neuro-science and Psychoanalysis took place in London in July 2000. The speakers included Antonio

Damasio, Oliver Sacks and Mark Solms and at the end of the weekend a new discipline was born: that of neuro-psychoanalysis. The neuro-scientists present put forward some of the discoveries that are taking place in that exponentially exploding field into the systemic workings of the mind/brain related to emotion/feeling/mood. One of the great contributions of psychoanalysis is the concept of *repetition compulsion* in its encapsulation of much that is tragic but also heroic in the human condition. What happens in the brain of a human being at these times is susceptible to being corroborated neuro-scientifically. Jung already explored the related theory of complexes in his early years in psychiatry with the word-association test. An extension of this may be to explore the way they correlate with the networking functioning of the brain.

The Overall Influence of Carl Gustav Jung

The prospective note at the end of the last chapter points us forward to researching the ways that Jung has had an impact on the world of psychotherapy and beyond. The take-up of his ideas has been widespread and every major figure in twentieth-century intellectual history refers to him. For instance, the founder of the behavioural movement, J.B. Watson, wrote a major criticism of *Psychological Types*. This book, along with *Symbols of Transformation*, was a bestseller in the USA.

The broadcasting of Jung's ideas through his books has been one way that analytical psychology has played a key role in the evolution of twentieth-century psychotherapy. There are others and the professionalization of analytical psychology is a major way in which it has spread its influence around the world.

The Professionalization of Analytical Psychology

The professionalization of analytical psychology follows the historical evolution of all such movements which start with a charismatic figure leading a group of like-minded adherents. This might be called the vocational stage when the leader's vision is shared by the first generation of disciples. The next important stage is the increasing coherence of the group and the setting up of a meeting place such as a club where like-minded people can foregather. As the enterprise begins to take on a more professional status, there is a growing need for some sort of demarcation in order to determine who are insiders and who outsiders. This leads to a need for greater institutionalization, which is followed by the setting up of training institutions and the putting in place of rules and regulations.

This was the pattern that analytical psychology followed, although due to Jung's much-vaunted dislike of institutions, the first training institutes did not come into being until after the Second World War and the founding of an international body, the International Association for Analytical Psychology (IAAP), which held its inaugural meeting in 1958.

The Separation of Analytical Psychology from Psychoanalysis

Zurich was an early centre for psychoanalysis and by 1912 a Psychoanalytical Association was in place that was connected to the Burghölzli Hospital and the University of Zurich. In 1912 the Zurich Psychoanalytical Association became an independent organization in separating from the Burghölzli and, in 1914, from the International Psychoanalytical Association (IPA). From this time on, psychoanalysis and analytical psychology developed along their separate paths. The stated intention of the Zurich analytical psychologists in leaving the IPA was that they wanted to be free of what they saw as dogmatism and the authority of one man – Freud.

The Zurich society was renamed the Association for Analytical Psychology and consisted, on the whole, of medical members who met once a week until 1918. At this time, it merged with the Analytical Psychology Club.

The Zurich Analytical Psychology Club

In 1913, the wealthy American, Edith Rockefeller McCormick, came to Zurich to be analysed by Jung and she increasingly began to practise as an analyst herself. It was due to a large financial donation from her that the first Analytical Psychology Club was founded in Zurich in 1916. According to Shamdasani, this was a lavishly furnished establishment that included a hostess, a cook, three servants and a workman (1998b: 21). The Club housed a consulting room, library, residential accommodation and a dining room and combined professional as well as social activities like billiards. Jung's intention behind founding the Club was to overcome the restrictions of one-to-one analysis and he wrote to Alphonse Maeder – whom he wanted to be the first president – that 'the experiment must be made' (1998b: 25).

Jung's interests were broadening around this time and he was developing a general psychology as evidenced by his book *Psychological Types*, which was being written around the same time. 'If the Club for Jung was an experiment that had to be made, its outcome and enduring legacy was *Psychological Types*' (Shamdasani, 1998b: 27). There were, therefore, two goals in Jung's mind when he decided to found the Club; these goals were based on professional and psychological aims.

The Club was inaugurated on 26 February 1916, with formal statutes and an executive committee that included Emma Jung as the chair, while Jung never served on the executive, remaining always an ordinary member. The Club was for both professional and lay members but there was a quite separate meeting for professionals only and Jung was always aware that the two constituencies had quite different purposes. As he said about analysts: 'They are people who are vitally interested in psychology while the lay people often merely indulge in a sort of lazy curiosity' (Shamdasani, 1998b: 40).

Jung's views on the establishment of an 'analytical collectivity' are expressed in a handwritten circular letter. He says that one tendency is characterized by a rigorous conception of the principles of analysis; the other is characterized by the emergence of ordinary familiarity and social gathering. This gives rise to difficulties as the two tendencies live in a state of opposition to one another – a certain amount of which is an inevitable part of living but super-fluous friction is to be avoided. He, therefore, advocated a better separation of both groups in the future with different floors reserved for each but allowing for mutual interaction. It was along this divide, in various parts of the world, that the professional wing of the Jungian movement always separated itself from lay members who would remain housed in the clubs. This was almost always a painful experience as the latter felt devalued.

A fascinating contribution to Jung's sixtieth birthday Festschrift volume by Emil Medtner, who was present at the inaugural meeting of the Club, is worth quoting here. Medtner was an important figure in the Russian symbolist movement and started an analysis with Jung in 1914. His article begins by saying that the idea of a psychological Club is so anti-Freudian that its existence alone would suffice as a demarcation between the two approaches. He goes on to say that outsiders imagine the relationship of Jung to the Club to be that of 'an occult master, an ideological leader . . . the director of a school or even the head doctor of an insane asylum for already convalescing neurotics' (Shamdasani, 1998b: 79). Far from this being the case, Medtner goes on to say that: 'Jung is the first who would be pleased if it could be established that the Club, without becoming untrue to his idea as a psychological Club, did not let itself be taken in tow by him' (Shamdasani, 1998b: 79). He also commends Jung's prowess at billiards!

The Zurich model was the one that repeated itself around the world with the starting point for analytical psychology in each city beginning with the founding of an Analytical Psychology Club.

The merger in 1918 of the Association for Analytical Psychology with the Analytical Psychology Club led to regular lectures taking place and these, combined with analysis, were the training ground for the first generation of Jungian analysts. Most of the latter saw both Jung and Toni Wolff for analysis so that an analysand would have a session with Jung on one day and with Wolff on the next.

Those analysts who had this experience said that he was excellent for archetypal work but Wolff was better on personal issues.

The C.G. Jung Institute was founded in 1948 but it was only with the establishing of the IAAP that the requirement for becoming an analyst ceased to depend on having analysis with Jung followed by a letter of recommendation from him.

The International Association for Analytical Psychology (IAAP)

This section is partly based on Thomas Kirsch's account in *The Jungians*. According to Jung's close associate, C.A. Meier, on Jung's 55th birthday in 1930, some of his close associates in Zurich persuaded him to think of forming an international professional organization. The International Association for Analytical Psychology (IAAP) was founded in that year and was structured according to Swiss law.

Its founding aims were to promote analytical psychology; to accredit professional groups and individual members where the former did not exist; and to hold regular congresses. The aims and structures of the IAAP have, of course, evolved over time. The first president of the IAAP was Robert Moody, who was a member of the Society of Analytical Psychology in London, and the first international congress was held in 1958. This event happens every three years and at the first six international congresses the predominant number of attendants was made up of Swiss and British analysts. The first international congress to be held outside Europe was in 1980 in San Francisco.

In 1980, the IAAP allocated funds to establish an annual newsletter, which came to serve as an important form of communication within the increasingly international community of the IAAP – at the time of writing, this includes 34 worldwide organizations with others in the process of being formed.

Funds were also provided to set up a research committee some years ago. This is currently conducting research into the efficacy of analytical psychology in Berlin, San Francisco and Zurich, where major projects are under way.

The IAAP has played a significant role in establishing analytical psychology as an international profession and the current president is the Italian analytical psychologist, Luigi Zoja.

The Americanization of Jung

The American connection was important for Jung from 1909 when he paid his first visit there with Freud and Ferenczi and Jung fell in love with the country. Part of that story has already been covered in Chapter 1, so this section will look at Jung's specific experience of the USA and of how his influence continued to burgeon there, in one way or the other, throughout the century. Eugene Taylor's book *Shadow Culture: Psychology and Spirituality in America*, will be referred to in order to give some of the background to Jung's experience in the USA.

As a result of the word-association test, Jung had by 1909 gained an international reputation and the Swiss-born pathologist Adolf Meyer, working in the asylums in New York State, had introduced Jung's work into the psychological literature. Meyer had been a student of Auguste Forel, who had held the Chair at the Burghölzli Hospital in Zurich before Bleuler and so Jung's work had entered the USA through his Swiss connections.

Taylor takes a similar view to Shamdasani in saying that many of Jung's ideas came from the 'French-Swiss-English-American alliance' (Taylor, 1999: 213). These included the *collective unconsciousness*, the comparative study of trance and mediumistic states and psychological types. In due course, many American physicians visited the Burghölzli Hospital; these included A.A. Brill, August Hoch and Frederick Peterson. Prominent Americans like Harold Fowler McCormick and Edith Rockefeller McCormick came to him as patients as did Fanny Bowditch, the daughter of the dean of Harvard Medical School.

After the first joint trip with Freud to the USA in 1909, Jung returned several times. His next visit was in 1910 when he passed through New York *en route* to Chicago to consult with the McCormicks. In 1912 Smith Ely Jeliffe arranged for him to lecture at Fordham University where Jung presented his own theories, which were published later as *Symbols of Transformation*. While he was in New York, he held seminars for psychiatrists at many institutions about which the *New York Times* printed a long story.

In 1913 he visited the USA for the last time before the First World War and did not return for 12 years, during which time a Jung circle began to form in New York. More will be said about this later in the chapter where I deal with the institutionalization of the Jungian movement. Jung returned to the USA in 1924 when he visited New York, Chicago, the Grand Canyon, Taos in New Mexico, New Orleans and Washington, D.C.

Two key figures in the history of American Jungian psychology were Henry Murray and Christiana Morgan. Murray was a physician and Melville scholar; Morgan a lay analyst and artist. Murray was a polymath and introduced psychoanalysis into academic psychology and literary criticism and the Thematic Apperception

Test into clinical practice. Morgan was a beautiful and intelligent woman from a Boston Brahmin family on her mother's side and a medical background on her father's. Her trance visions helped her gain access to the deepest recesses of her feminity and the notebooks she kept formed the basis of Jung's Vision Seminars.

Although they were both married to other people, they embarked on an erotic, religious and intellectual quest together for 40 years, which devastated others and left many of their own aspirations unfulfilled. 'They were both guilty of being too rich, too privileged, too narcissistic, and too absorbed in the overblown spiritual import-ance of their essentially illicit relationship' (Taylor, 1999: 225).

Murray's influence enabled Jung to return to the USA in 1936 and on this occasion he received an honorary doctorate from Harvard University. Towards the end of his life, Jung came to feel somewhat embittered towards the USA as he eventually became overshadowed there by Freud. This was due to the fact that in the late 1930s, with the growing threat of Nazism in Europe, many psychoanalysts fled to the USA. Due to their influence, psychoanalysis increasingly infiltrated the American medical establishment and was in control of clinical teaching in psychology and psychiatry until recent times.

Humanistic and Transpersonal Psychology
The dominance in the USA of psychoanalysis, on the one hand, and behaviourism, which controlled academic teaching departments of psychology, on the other, brought about a reaction in the 1940s and 1950s that culminated in the humanistic movement. This thrived between 1941 and 1969 in the academy attracting scholars from the humanities and social sciences. With the social and political upheavals of the late 1960s, humanistic psychology split into three parts, one of which was transpersonal psychology.

One of the catalyst figures in the evolution of the new psychology was Abraham Maslow. He was a New Yorker who taught at Columbia and Brooklyn College, where he came in contact with the psychoanalysts Karen Horney and Erich Fromm. He only began to develop his own controversial ideas after the Second World War, which culminated in what he called 'self-actualizing' and applied to individuals who were able to achieve the highest and best of their potential.

Maslow's ideas came together with those of Anthony Sutich from Palo Alto, who was completely incapacitated by an accident and spent most of his life in a supine position. During his long periods of immobilization, he noticed that people came to talk to him about their problems and to seek his advice and this led to him deciding to become a psychotherapist.

In 1949, Sutich and Maslow met for the first time and found that they shared an interest in growth-oriented psychology. They also had many colleagues with similar views and these included Rollo May, Carl Rogers, Margaret Mead and Gregory Bateson. It was the coming together of Maslow and Sutich that led to the founding of Transpersonal Psychology in the late 1960s and they counted amongst their godfathers William James because of his exploration of mystical consciousness in *The Varieties of Religious Experience*. The term 'transpersonal' was inspired by James, who had used it during a Harvard course.

Maslow and Sutich also counted Jung as a predecessor as they recognized elements of transpersonal psychology in his emphasis on *archetypes* and the *transcendent function*. Sutich launched the transpersonal movement in 1969 from northern California and its studies included phenomena like self-actualizing and transcendence.

> In California, humanistic and transpersonal psychologists have woven psychoanalysis around gender issues, theories and politics, with Jung having superseded Freud as the new guru of inner exploration, where meditation and transcendence take center stage with spiritual development in the therapeutic encounter. (Taylor, 1998: 111)

Maslow, in his turn, was elected to the presidency of the American Psychological Association, which gave the establishment's seal of approval to the humanistic and transpersonal psychology movement.

The New Age Movement is also said to have adopted Jung as one of its godfathers. According to a 1998 book, *New Age Religion and Western Culture: Esotericism in the Mirror of Secular Thought*, by the Dutch religious scholar, Wouter J. Hanegraaff, the ideas underlying this movement are Gnostic, Neoplatonist, alchemical, hermetic and occultist. These would, of course, have a great affinity with many of Jung's ideas. However, Taylor is critical of this thesis and says it describes the European New Age not the specifically American one, which traces its unique character back to American religious consciousness.

Formative Impact of Jung's Seminal Ideas

Many of Jung's ideas have passed into everyday usage – *extravert* and *introvert* are two that were mentioned in the Introduction. Others have been taken up and applied by psychiatry and psychology. This section will look in greater depth at those that have had a pervading influence. Some of the major ones have already been elaborated at length in preceding chapters such as alchemy, *active imagination*, dream interpretation, psychic energy, the *numinous*, the *transcendent function*, teleology, Trickster, complexes and *anima/animus* amongst others. I will elaborate below some of Jung's other ideas that I am most frequently asked about, most of which have taken root in the collective consciousness one way or the other.

Archetypes

Throughout the book there has been mention of Jung's concept of archetypes and links have been made to the important sources that he drew from in developing this part of his ideas system. Briefly, they are the inherited part of the psyche that gives rise to patterned tendencies of thought. The American analytical psychologist, Murray Stein's definition of the actual term archetype is that *typos* means stamp and *arche* means the original or master copy. Thus the psyche carries the mark of the archetype.

Bi-polarity is inherent in archetypes and three archetypal pairings will be illustrated in order to flesh out Jung's schema, in the course of which reference is made to definitions in John Beebe's classificatory system.

The archetype of the *hero/heroine* or *persona* is opposed to the *shadow* or opposing personality. The definition of persona is that it represents that aspect of an individual which is in relation to the outer world. It derives from the Greek word for 'mask' and denotes those masks that were worn by actors in performing comic/tragic parts in Greek plays. The less acceptable parts of the personality are kept hidden behind the persona. A well-differentiated person develops a well-fitting persona and the latter is essential for survival. Each individual has to deal with a variety of situations in the course of the day, for instance, being with loved ones, meeting the bank manager, managing a career, etc. An individual who cannot put on the right clothes for each occasion is at a disadvantage and may even be at risk – think of Marilyn Monroe in this context.

The hero/heroine is often synonymous with the persona and Beebe suggests Heracles as the embodiment of the hero. On the other hand, Odysseus was a cunning ambiguous sort of hero who often lied and cheated and for this reason he may be identified with the *wounded hero* – i.e. one who bears the marks of his imperfections and may be equated with the therapist, who is able consciously to bear their vulnerabilities. For this reason, Odysseus and the *Odyssey* are linked with Jungian therapy which holds the archetype of the *wounded healer* in a central position containing as it does the opposites of healing/fallibility.

The shadow has already been elaborated in the course of the book but it is important to bear in mind that there is a personal shadow that is the repository of all the aspects of an individual that they are ashamed about and in denial of. There is also *archetypal shadow*, which is identified with the dark side of the self, which is here treated as an archetype. It is this archetypal shadow that Jung was referring to when he talked about the existence of evil.

The next pairing is the *wise old man or woman* which is opposed to the *senex or witch*. The first part of the pairing is synonymous with the Good Father or Mother as portrayed in myths and fairytales – the former as Zeus, the latter as Mary or Demeter. This good parent nurtures and guides the person and is also an internal one being identified with positive aspects of the self. This may function in a quite unconscious way in an individual, acting to direct one away from a consciously driven position that is seen in retrospect to have been the better way. For instance, many people are 'directed' in this way to come into therapy and say when they first arrive that they have no idea why they are there.

The opposite of the above, the senex/witch, is constellated in the image of the Terrible Father or Mother – there is a positive aspect to senex but what is being alluded to here is the dark side. Kronos, the Greek Titan, who ate his children and who foreshadows Herod's slaughter of the innocents, is an example of the former. Kali, the creator/destroyer Terrible Mother, or the Medusa, the icy-cold petrifier, are examples of the latter. It is the witch's voice that undermines an individual by whispering in their ear that they are hopeless and the pathological manifestation of this archetype is depression. The senex/witch is against all life and attacks both the soul and the spirit, however, Beebe also points to another aspect, which is its power to prick inflation and to act as an obstacle that may steer one in a more creative direction.

The third pairing is the *puer/puella* which is opposed by the *Trickster*. The former signifies the eternal creativity of youth and is represented in myth as the birth of the divine child. Its attributes are spirituality, creativity, new beginnings and enthusiasm. The negative of this is remaining immature and irresponsible and being ungrounded. Many patients coming into Jungian therapy are caught in this archetype, as instanced by the individual who comes to a Jungian analyst seeking a mystical experience. The analytic task here will be concentrated on grounding such an individual through increasing ego strength while not damaging the creativity that comes from the puer/puella. What can happen in this kind of analytic encounter is that the patient and analyst may become polarized with the former identifying with the eternal youth and the latter becoming identified with the negative *senex*.

Narcissus is the god associated with the puer/puella and Icarus the mythological personification who, flying too close to the sun – in other words being inflated and ungrounded – melted his wings held together with wax and crashed down to earth.

The Trickster has been encountered in the section above on alchemy and is synonymous with Hermes/Mercurius who can be both treacherous and humorous in enabling one to laugh at oneself. The Court Jester was a living example of the Trickster, who through wit and humour could tell the King painful home truths. The Trickster is above all the mediator and can bring the puer/puella into greater consciousness.

Collective Unconscious

Jung distinguishes between a *personal unconscious*, which is the repository of personal memories, repressed painful ideas and contents that are not yet ready to reach consciousness. He equates this with the personal shadow. The other kind of unconsciousness is of a quite different order and Jung called this the *collective unconscious*. This is the realm of the archetypes and of the ancient and universal 'thought-forms'which are common to all humans. It is here that can be found the 'hidden treasure upon which mankind ever and anon has drawn, and from which it has raised up its gods and demons' (Jung, 1953b: 66).

It is from the collective unconscious that everything irrational proceeds, whereas all rational contents are tied to the conscious mind. It is from this primordial realm that the challenge is thrown down as if by an interior enemy to the conscious attitude of the individual. In Jungian therapy the first task is usually concentrated on the personal parental images but once these have been worked through the real work begins on the archetypal parental images that belong to the realm of the collective unconscious. Jung felt that this latter task belonged in the second-half of life, i.e. after the mid-30s, and he says: 'No wonder that many bad neuroses appear at the onset of life's afternoon. It is a sort of second puberty, another "storm and stress" period, not infrequently accompanied by tempests of passion – the "dangerous age"' (Jung, 1953b: 75).

This situation is often repeated in the therapist's consulting room in both positive and negative ways. For instance, there is the person in their mid-50s who has never rebelled in youth and lives it in later life with the spouse/partner and family as the negative authority figures that must be overthrown. It may also be the time when a woman who has spent her life in service to parents/husband/children may be gripped by the sort of archetypal energy that can lead her on to a new path of career or relationship.

When . . . psychic energy regresses, going beyond even the period of early infancy, and breaks into the legacy of ancestral life, the mythological images are awakened: these are the archetypes. An interior spiritual world whose existence we never suspected opens out and displays contents which seem to stand in sharpest contrast to all our former ideas. (Jung, 1953b: 77)

These contents give rise to such intense feelings that millions may be captivated by them; here Jung cites the modern Gnostic systems of theosophy and anthroposophy because Christianity, unlike these two syncretistic movements, is incapable of attaining the richness of pagan symbolism which speaks to the powerful contents in the collective unconscious.

Archetypes and Instincts

The American analytical psychologist, Murray Stein, has given an excellent account of the relationship between archetypes and instincts in his 1998 book, *Jung's Map of the Soul*. Although the two belong together, Stein states that Jung was not trying to reduce one to the other. Psyche exists in the space between pure body and transcendent mind and consciousness struggles 'in a regular panic against being swallowed up in the primitivity and unconsciousness of sheer instinctuality' (Stein, 1998: 101).

However, psyche also resists being taken over by the transcendent end of the spectrum and so fluctuates between the instinctual pole and the archetypal spiritual pole. 'Jung maps the psyche as a spectrum, with the archetype at the ultraviolet end and the instinct at the infrared end' (Stein, 1998: 102). What usually happens in practice is that the two interact in the unconscious and unite to produce energized manifestations in consciousness such as ideas, strivings and urges. These two polarized opposites are located at either end of the psyche and it is there that lies the *psychoid*, or beyond psyche, areas which give rise to psychosomatic symptoms and parapsychological phenomena.

Information from beyond the psyche passes from the psychoid realm into that of the collective unconscious and from there may surface into consciousness. 'The burden of choice is placed on ego-consciousness to deal ethically with these invasions from inner space' (Stein, 1998: 103).

The Self

The self is the pivotal centre of Jung's conception of the psyche and like his other key contributions it is one that he experienced first and later incorporated into his theoretical framework. For him, the self transcends the psychic realm, that is, it goes beyond and even defines it. Jung's encounter with the self occurred during the years 1916–18 in the difficult time that followed his break with Freud in 1913. In the course of those two years he had direct experience of what he came to see as the bedrock of psychological wholeness, that which both keeps the psyche from falling apart at times of great stress but also transcends and goes beyond the psyche. He termed this the self.

Jung fully elaborated his notions of the self in his 1951 book *Aion*, which represents the collective aspect of the individuation process. It starts with simple definitions of the ego and the self where Jung warns of the danger of the former being assimilated by the latter. This results in the image of wholeness remaining in the unconscious as it is from the self that all ideas of wholeness and unity emanate. If the self is assimilated to the ego this results in inflation and grandiosity of the latter.

The term Aion denotes an historical period of time and, in the book, Jung explores psychological development related to different signs in the Zodiac. For instance, the period from 0 to 2000 AD is the time of the fishes – the first thousand years being the time of Christ and the second thousand the time of the Anti-Christ. It is in this way that Jung related individual psychic development to what is in the collective psyche of any particular time. The symbols of the self are different at different historical epochs and like everything in life, symbols have their day and cease to be.

Jung says that the self is a true 'complexio oppositorum' and has a paradoxical character. In this way, it is male and female, old and young, powerful and helpless, divine and demonic. It is both the totality of psyche and also the agent in its manifestation as the archetypal urge to co-ordinate, relativize and mediate the tension of the opposites. For Jung, the self is *the* organizing principle of the unconscious.

As Jung's personal encounter with the unifying power of the self happened in mid-life, he went on to theorize that this is experienced in the same way by everyone. As we saw in the section to do with Michael Fordham, the latter disputed this claim and went on to formulate his own theory of self.

Individuation

Jung's term *individuation* applies to a deep inner coming together that symbolizes the union of consciousness with the unconscious. The figure of the *androgyne* has been cited as signifying this union that brings about a great increase in consciousness and an expansion of the personality.

Andrew Samuels, Bani Shorter and Fred Plaut's definition of individuation from their book, *A Critical Dictionary of Jungian Analysis* will be partly referred to. Jung took the term from Schopenhauer but it originates with Gerard Dorn, a sixteenth-century alchemist.

Paradoxically, on the one hand, individuation means becoming wholly and indivisibly oneself in distinction to others but, on the other, it also means gathering the world to oneself in order to fulfil collective qualities more completely and satisfactorily. What it definitely does *not* mean is any advocating of individualism or narcissism on the part of the person. Jung was himself an introvert and made most of his discoveries at a time of great introversion from 1913–18, which has led to interpreting him as giving greater value to the inner as opposed to the outer world. Even amongst some Jungian practitioners it is clearly thought to be 'good' to be an introvert as opposed to an extravert with the consequent advocating of a narcissistic withdrawal from the world. This is not what Jung meant by individuation.

There are real dangers involved in the individuation process, one being the sort of inflation pointed to in the paragraph above. The other is that the path to *individuating* entails confrontation with the powerful forces that lie in the unconscious which, if not handled carefully, can lead to depression or even a psychotic episode. It is vital for anyone setting off on this path to build up sufficient ego-strength to try to ensure that they can withstand emanations from the unconscious realm.

To continue in this vein, it is as important to define what individuation is not as it is to point to what it is. It is, for instance, often confused with *integration* but is, in fact, quite different from it. Briefly, integration is ego-driven and relates to an expansion of consciousness through the assimilation of the personal shadow and the working through of ego-defences like *denial, projection, repression*, etc.

The individuation process is driven by the self and its motivating force is Jung's concept of *compensation*, which is the fundamental motivating principle between consciousness and the unconscious. As has already been said in another part of this book, once the ego achieves sufficient autonomy, there is a tendency on its part to want to forget its 'lowly' origins in the unconscious. This can lead to a split with the ego becoming dissociated from the unconscious followed by concomitant neurotic symptoms. Although these appear in a negative form, they are harbingers of the individuation process which, if attended to, can lead to the healing of the split. Jung was known to have said of someone: 'Thank God he became neurotic.' This is the psyche's way of signalling that there is an imbalance between consciousness and the unconscious and the consequent need for greater balance.

At this point, people often come into therapy and, in the Jungian approach, the analyst is as much in the therapy as the patient. This was illustrated in the section on the archetypal transference/countertransference and alchemy. Images of the self will manifest at this time as contents from the collective unconscious begin to invade the conscious mind. These may appear in dreams in the form of *mandalas*, which take the shape of a circle enclosed by a square and which occur in the religion and art of many diverse cultures. They also appear frequently in alchemy. The process once started is likely to take a long time and this is the reason why an in-depth Jungian analysis is of lengthy duration. The question that is increasingly asked is whether long analyses are necessary or even beneficial. Jung's answer is as follows: '. . . small and invisible as the contribution may be it is yet a *magnum opus* . . . The ultimate questions of psychotherapy are not a private matter – they represent a supreme responsibility' (Jung, 1954: 234).

The Stages of Life

For Jung, the individuation process was linked to the second half of life so it is important to give an outline of what he meant by the stages of life. He divides these into two and posits that the first half stretches from puberty to somewhere between 35 and 40 years old. Prior to that, childhood is a time of complete dependence on parents and it is as though the child is not yet completely born but remains still enclosed in the psychic space of its parents. As we saw above, this was contested by Michael Fordham from his considerable experience of working with children.

The tasks of the first half of life include the separation from the mother and the development of a strong ego. This comes about by acquiring an adult identity in a variety of ways that includes forming relationships, possibly culminating in a permanent pairing with another and/or producing children. The development of oneself as a social being is also the task of this life stage through further education, pursuing a career and the establishment of a way of life.

The transition to the second half of life appeared always traumatic to Jung and is accompanied by depression in men around 40 years old but somewhat earlier in women. This theory, along with his one on the development of the self, was clearly influenced by his personal experiences. For him, the goals of the second half of life are different to the first which are orientated to outer achievement. In the second half, the libido changes direction and is orientated inwards to the unification of the ego with the unconscious. It is here that a person's unrealized potential lies in the increasing opening up of the ego-self axis. According to Jung, the second stage is also the time of preparation for death.

While finding Jung's two life stages somewhat limiting, I think his hypothesis contains the seeds of a creative way of thinking about life as a series of stages to be negotiated. Through increasing experience of working with individuals in therapy, I have come to see that there are in fact many 'stages of life' and I invariably find that a person has come into therapy expressing feelings about 'being stuck'. This usually means that they are caught in that liminal place between one stage and the next. It is this liminal space that Murray Stein so aptly identifies with Hermes when everything is in flux and giving rise to anxiety and panic attacks.

My own thinking has for a long time concentrated on the vital significance of rites of passage rather than life stages, as it is at these times of fluidity that rituals are needed and therapy is above all *the* ritual of modern and postmodern times. I conceptualize the whole of a long therapy as a major rite of passage, with each session as a minor one entailing, as it does, a rite of entry, followed by the ritual that takes place in the course of the session and, finally, the rite of exit when the person has to put on the appropriate persona in order to face the outer world.

The most profound rite of passage for a woman is the one associated with working through the menopause. This is often accompanied by experiences of social death, for instance the loss of a spouse/partner, children leaving home and the fear of being less attractive. If this rite of passage can be successfully worked through, it can open up the way to the most productive stage for a woman in which she can at last come into her own and take control of her individual life.

Synchronicity

Jung was a border raider *par excellence* and he loved nothing better than pushing at the edges of what is already known. Murray Stein's work will be used as the reference point for Jung's theory of *synchronicity*. As Stein says, Jung's theorizing about the psychoid led him to develop a single unified system that not only encapsulated both matter and spirit but also created a link between time and eternity.

Random events, chance and chaos held a fascination for him and he noted that they often display a meaning for which there is no causal explanation. For him the hexagrams of 'I Ching', in the *Chinese Book of Changes*, sometimes display a pattern of meaning that can link current events to an unfolding pattern in the future. It was to try to throw light on how these meaningful patterns can happen without a known cause that Jung embarked on his theory of synchronicity, what may be thought of as meaningful coincidence or an 'acausal connecting principle'.

An example of this kind of synchronization of inner and outer events is an incident he experienced in a session with a patient. The latter had a dream of a gold scarab beetle which they were discussing in Jung's study when there was a noise at the window, which turned out to be a local version of the beetle trying to get into the room. Jung inferred from incidents like this that archetypal images in dreams may coincide with outer events. His explanation was that as archetypes are not limited to the psychic realm they can transgress boundaries and manifest in the outer world. Jung applied the term synchronicity when inner and outer simultaneously come together. Jung conjectured that synchronicity often occurs when there is an *abaissement du niveau mental* – a sort of lowering of consciousness – at which time unconscious contents become more active.

The *Collected Works* have many references and allusions to the *unus mundus* – the unified cosmos – and to the idea of synchronicity and Jung collaborated with the Nobel Prize-winning physicist, Wolfgang Pauli, to explore a possible relationship between nature and psyche. Jung also published an essay: 'Synchronicity: An Acausal Connecting Principle', to elucidate his thesis that: 'There is a dimension in which psyche and world intimately interact with and reflect one another' (Stein, 1998: 202).

In this paper, Jung introduces the idea that synchronicity, along with space/time and causality, may be a new paradigm that can be used to give a complete account of reality as it is experienced by human beings and measured by scientists. In this way, he brings the psyche into the forefront of reality by stating that 'the meaningful coincidence between a psychic event and an objective event' must be taken into account.

Jung was aware that the kind of perspective he was proposing makes huge demands on the Western mind, which thinks along strictly rational lines and, as Stein himself says: 'The Age of Enlightenment left a legacy of facticity without meaning' (Stein, 1998: 216). The key word there is *meaning* and Jung's point is that the question of meaning requires answers that do not solely take into account the causal sequence of events. Along with Pauli, he worked out a diagram to try to do just that. It is in the form of a cross with the vertical line meeting with the horizontal in the middle. Along its vertical spine runs the space/time continuum and along its horizontal arm the causality/synchronicity continuum. The advantage of this model is 'that it makes possible a view which includes the psychoid factor in our description and knowledge of nature – that is, an a priori meaning or "equivalence"' (Stein, 1998: 216).

Jung had to expand his theory of the nonpsychic nature of archetypes in order to bring them into line with synchronistic events that transgress the boundaries of the psychic world. For this reason, he introduced the idea of the *transgresivity* of archetypes to cover that aspect of them that goes beyond the psychic and can occur in the physical world. This term points to the idea that patterns that occur in the psyche are related to those that lie outside of it: 'the archetypes are not found exclusively in the psychic sphere but can occur just as much in circumstances that are not psychic' (Stein, 1998: 218).

Stein speculates as to how this might be applied to a coming together of instinct and archetype. For instance, a sexual instinct might become activated by causal events i.e. genetic factors and early childhood experiences and also because an archetypal field has been constellated. In this way, a chance encounter might turn into a life-long relationship.

> Why such connections take place seems a mystery if we reflect only upon causality, but if we introduce the synchronistic factor and the dimension of meaning we come closer to a more complete and satisfying answer . . . Falling into the archetypal world of synchronistic events feels like living in the will of God. (Stein, 1998: 219)

Typology

Typology, as Jung developed it, has already been elaborated as an historical and theoretical construct in Chapter 3. On reading *Psychological Types*, the long book that is devoted to typology, one is struck by the fact that nine-tenths of it are devoted to historical associations. The reason for this is that, in Jung's view, psychology had to be historical in order to be relevant. The return to typology in this section is to illustrate a couple of revisions of it as a theory and to demonstrate its application in two different ways.

It would be in order to revisit the basic assumptions that underlie the theory which states that there are two attitudes – extraversion and introversion – and four functions – thinking, feeling, intuition and sensation. The first two of these are the rational functions and the second two the non-rational ones. Jung went on to postulate that the superior function had its opposing inferior function in the one at the other end of a vertical spine. So that if an individual's superior way of functioning was thinking their inferior function would be feeling. If these two are polarized opposite each other on a vertical spine, then the other two non-rational functions would be along a horizontal arm with, say, sensation as the auxiliary and intuition as the tertiary function. Added to each of these would be their associated attitudes of extraversion or introversion.

Beebe's model proposes a second quaternity of functions that says that the first one is 'ego-syntonic' but the second is 'ego-alien'. This then gives eight functions for each individual. He further proposes that if a function is extraverted its opposite will be introverted. Beebe came upon this way of conceptualizing as a result of a great deal of experience of typological analysis.

In order to clarify this model, let us look at each set of four as follows. In the 'ego-syntonic' quarternity there is first *extraverted thinking* as the superior function; opposite is the fourth *introverted feeling* function along the vertical spine; the horizontal arm carries, on one side the auxiliary of *introverted sensation* and, on the other, the tertiary *extraverted sensation* function.

In the 'ego-alien' quaternity, the attitudes associated with each of the functions will be inverted as follows: introverted thinking as the fifth function at the top of the spine with extraverted feeling as the eighth at the bottom. *Extraverted sensation* is the sixth function at one end of the arm and *introverted intuition* at the other end as the seventh function.

Beebe links these eight to his archetypal pairings that were outlined in the section above. For instance, in the 'ego-syntonic' quaternity delineated above, the superior function of extraverted thinking would link to the archetype of the hero/heroine and would be the consciously achieving function. As it is the closest to consciousness, it would be closely related to the individual's ego and persona.

The introverted thinking function is still closely related to the individual's conscious identity but because of its introverted orientation, it is closer to the self than the superior extraverted thinking.

The second or auxiliary function is related to the archetypal pairing of the Good Mother/Father and will be used by the individual to take care of others. The third fuction is linked to the puer/puella pairing and will be a source of creativity. The 'ego-syntonic' quarternity continues on in this vein.

Let us turn now to the 'ego-alien' quaternity and look at the fifth function, which is the shadow of the hero/heroine. This opposes the individual's heroic myth and results in a refusal to get into life. The example Beebe gives is of Achilles sulking in his tent as this opposing personality manifests in passive–aggression, suspiciousness, avoidance, etc.

The sixth function is identified with the witch/senex archetype and is the negative parent that attacks the person relentlessly in a shadowy underhand manner telling them that they are hopeless, stupid and will never get anywhere. The seventh function lines up with the Trickster, which fools and confuses the individual and others in their vicinity. It manifests as what Gregory Bateson called double-binding where an enforced choice always results in getting it wrong; or a confusing of Matte-Blanco's with asymmetrical thinking.

Lastly, comes the *Daimonic/Demonic* eighth function which can completely subvert the individual and others. This is such a vitally important theme it is worth elaborating it further. The American existential psychologist, Rollo May, used the classical Greek idea of the *daimon* to depict any natural function which has the power to take over the person. Examples of this are sex, the craving for power and rage. The daimonic is at the creative pole and the demonic at the destructive pole.

May is, of course, talking about an archetypal way of functioning and it was this that Jung encountered at the time of his descent into the unconscious in the daimonic figures of Philemon, Salome and the serpent. These figures from the collective unconscious were Jung's guides into the depths of his psyche and to a relationship with the powers that lie hidden there. It was thought by some scholars that in antiquity Plato and Homer used the term daimon as though it were synonymous with God. This is disputed by scholars who say that daimon alludes to something amorphous, indeterminate and incorporeal; whereas *theos* referred to the personification of a god like Zeus or Apollo.

Nevertheless, all that is daimonic lies between the mortal and the immortal and functions to communicate messages from the gods to humans. Beebe's own definition is as follows:

> The *daimon* refers to a deeply instinctive, archetypal part of personality that asserts itself autonomously as a force for good or evil (and often both) through its strongly delivered intentions that undermine the adaptation of the psyche in both destructive and creative ways. The *daimon's* style (on a continuum from raging to loving) defines the most problematic aspect of human character. It forms the built-in moral limit of any psyche, for it is the paradoxical dark spirit of the person's unconscious will, with which the person's soul (*anima/animus*) must struggle. Out of the encounter with the *daimon* emerges 'the problem of evil', because what is most difficult in character is also potentially what is most healing. In fact, the *daimon* is an autonomous spiritual complex that links the individual to divinity, itself a *complexio oppositorum* of light and dark energies. (Personal communication)

The creative outcome of Beebe's model of typology is that it brings together relational aspects with archetypal ones which may also be applied to the therapeutic situation. Beebe notes that if there is a marked difference in the therapist and patient's type profiles this will, most likely, result in a 'stormy, quarrelsome transference/countertransference' therapeutic relationship. What is worse, the two may become caught together in their demonic functions and the end result is the sort of therapy that goes tragically wrong for both parties. This applies equally to any other relationship – one has only to think of the horror stories that emanate from the divorce courts!

Myers–Briggs Type Indicator and the Diagnostic and Statistical Manual – III

A classificatory test used in psychology and one in psychiatry will be briefly investigated next; the first has many of Jung's original hypotheses built into it and the second is claimed to have strong affinities with them.

The typology test used in psychology is the Myers–Briggs Type Indicator (MBTI). This test led to a re-evaluating of an individual's typology in a systematic way by identifying three implications in Jung's original theory: one is the constant presence of the auxiliary function; second, the important result of combining perception and judgment – the MBTI terms that replaced 'rational' and 'irrational' in the original; and, lastly, the role of the auxiliary function in balancing extraversion–introversion.

The final scale of the test endeavours to show how a perceiving type orientates to life in a different way to a judging one. For instance, perceiving through sensing and intuiting is shown to lead to a flexible, spontaneous approach to life. Individuals who are primarily perceiving types will stay open to experience and be comfortable with their ability to adapt to the exigencies of the moment.

Individuals who are orientated to a more judging approach through thinking and feeling tend to live in a planned and orderly way and try to regulate and control their environment. They also tend to be structured and organized and decisions taken by them will lead to closure. It is important to bear in mind that 'judging' used in this context does not imply 'judgmental' as any of the types may be prone to the latter.

Jung himself originally connected typology with psychopathology and Soren Ekstrom's study of the Diagnostic and Statistical Manual–III (DSM–III) used in American psychiatry, linked this psychiatric classificatory system with Jung's typology. Ekstrom compared eight maladaptive traits described in *Psychological Types*, with eight characterological disorders in the DSM and found a striking degree of overlap. This study is to be found in Renos Papadopoulos (1992), which includes a critique of it, but Ekstrom holds firm to his thesis.

Sandplay

At the time of his confrontation with the unconscious, Jung went through a period of playing in sand along the shores of Lake Zurich. Sandplay grew out of that and is a form of *active imagination* and non-verbal therapy. A tray is utilized and has to be 28.5 × 19.5 inches with a depth of 3 inches and a height of 30. The inside is painted blue to signify sea or sky and two trays are provided – one filled with wet and the other with dry sand. According to Dora Maria Kalff, its founder in the 1950s, the tray is a 'free and protected space' (Kirsch, 2000: 233). The therapist is a participant observer in the process and may make interpretations but passes no judgment on the quality of the sand pictures.

Sandplay can be a means of evoking archetypal material that can open the way to analytical work; for others, it can be a way of freeing oneself from the need for language. Apart from being practised by a number of Jungian analysts, it has been taken up worldwide in a variety of arenas, including schools and family therapy and acts as a bridge between East and West. The distinguished Japanese Jungian analyst, Hayao Kawai, is a strong supporter of the technique and when I was in Japan in 1995, there were approximately 14 Jungian analysts, a few more psychoanalysts and more than 400 sandplay therapists.

The Academy and Research

Jung wrote books more than he propounded theories and his writing style may best be likened to quasi-automatism akin to the inspirational writing of Nietzsche's in *Ecce Homo*. One is aware when reading Jung that he starts off without any idea of where he is going and ends up far from his starting point. The fact that he is not interested in creating meta-narratives gives his writings a distinctly postmodern edge. On the other hand, what has worked against him in the academy is the non-secular bias of his psychology, which is unacceptable in a secular age. Jung shares in common with Nietzsche the fact that they are both what might be called 'psychologized Protestants'.

The situation is changing and there is a growing interest in Jung's ideas in academie as, increasingly, Jungian psychology is represented on university curricula.

Jung was himself a Professor at the National Scientific University in Zurich as was his successor, C.A. Meier. Currently, the analytical psychologist, Verena Kast, is an Associate Professor at the University of Zurich so that Jungian thought is represented on the curriculum there.

The University of Essex in the **UK**, where Renos Papadopoulos and Andrew Samuels jointly hold the Chair in Analytical Psychology, has established analytical psychology as an academic discipline. This writer is one of the team assembled by the two professors to offer tuition in postgraduate courses and the university produces public lectures and carries out research in analytical psychology.

The situation in the **USA** has already been touched on in the section above. In his book, *The Jungians*, Thomas Kirsch reports the following individuals being active in American academe. In 1941, the Jungian analyst, Joseph Wheelwright became an instructor at the Langley-Porter Neuropsychiatric Institute which is part of the University of California Medical Centre in San Francisco. He taught analytical psychology to psychiatric residents and psychologists for more than 30 years and many Jungian analysts have succeeded him as instructors at Langley-Porter.

Joseph Henderson followed a similar path at Stanford Medical School where he gave dream seminars to psychiatric residents for 15 years. When this School moved to Palo Alto, Thomas Kirsch continued the tradition of teaching for 30 years and there are many other Jungians on the staff of Stanford.

David Rosen is the first Professor in Analytical Psychology at the University of Texas where he and his students have been undertaking research projects and theses in analytical psychology.

Harry Wilmer, an academic psychiatrist and psychoanalyst, underwent a Jungian analysis and became an individual member of the IAAP in 1974. He took over the directorship of the Institute of Humanities in Salado, Texas, which now includes a forum for analytical psychology.

In **Australia** there are courses in analytical psychology at La Trobe University in Melbourne and Western Sydney University. David Tacey, Anne Brown and Peter Fullerton have put in place a masters degree programme at La Trobe.

In **Brazil** the Pontificia Universidade Católica de São Paulo's Psychology Department runs graduate and postgraduate courses in analytical psychology. At the graduate level these include fundamentals and basic concepts in diagnosis and therapy in analytical psychology as well as its theory and practice. At the postgraduate level, there are masters and PhD courses in analytical psychology and religion, and analytical psychology and clinical psychology. (Personal communication with Denise Ramos.)

In **France**, Christian Gaillard is a Professor at the Ecole Nationale Supérieure des Beaux-arts and in 1998 published his magnificent volume entitled *Le Musée imaginaire de Carl Gustav Jung*, bringing together his abiding interest in analytical psychology and art.

In Israel there are analytical psychology courses on offer in many of the major universities.

Henry Abramovitch has given postgraduate seminars on Dreams and The Father at the Sackler School of Medicine, Tel Aviv University. A number of analysts teach a similar programme at Haifa University.

Avi Baumann conducts postgraduate courses in analytical psychology at the Freud Center, Department of Psychology, Hebrew University.

Beni Mor and other analytical psychologists teach and supervise the training of art therapists at Leslie College, Netania and Boston.

The Head of Clinical Training and Student Counselling Service at Hebrew University is a recent analytical psychology graduate.

Micha Ankori teaches courses with a Jungian orientation in the Department of Psychology, Tel Aviv University.

There is also a three-year Diploma course in Analytical Psychology at the Kibbutz College, Tel Aviv. (Personal communication with Henry Abramovitch.)

In Japan, the Analytical Psychologist, Toshio Kawai holds the Chair in Clinical Psychology at the University of Kyoto and has incorporated many analytical psychology ideas into that course. Five years ago, I spent a short time working with him and his eminent father, the analytical psychologist, Hayao Kawai, in the Psychology Department at Kyoto University. Kawai Senior is the president of the International Research Studies Centre for Japanese Studies. There is also an analytical psychology postgraduate course at Konan University, Kobe, and one at Osaka University. (Personal communication with Toshio Kawai.)

In South Africa, the University of Rhodes offers a PhD course in psychotherapy which incorporates a module on analytical psychology. (Personal communication with Astrid Berg.)

This is not a comprehensive list of university courses in analytical psychology and is only meant as an indicator of the increasing take-up of Jungian ideas in the academy.

Multicultural

Two examples of how Jungian ideas are at work in widely differing cultures around the world will be given from *Post-Jungians Today*. The first is by the Brazilian analytical psychologist, Roberto Gambini, whose paper I summarized in the Introduction.

Brazil

The Challenge of Backwardness, by Roberto Gambini, is a profoundly moving but also disturbing account of the traumatic history of Brazil, a country belonging to what is called the developing world.

For Gambini, there is an imbalance in his country's psyche and he uses an in-depth synthesis of the archetypal, alchemical and astrological – which give so much meaning to the Jungian approach – to analyse Brazil. He turns to Jung's work, *Aion*, to point to the convergence of the Renaissance and the Discovery (Invasion) of Brazil by the Portuguese in 1500. The 'discovery' of the New World represents an archetypal encounter of two contrasting parts of humankind which culminated in the climax of its achievement for one culture and the loss of the ancestral soul for the other.

The alchemical synthesis that could have happened between European and Amerindian ways of being was replaced, instead, by the domination of one polarity over the other. Brazil has no myth of origin and the myths that belong to the indigenous people, to do with incest, hunger, danger, and meaning in life, have been completely subjugated to the dominant European ethos. It is now for the therapists to do the soul work of rehabilitating the mythology of their native land. This is part of the individuating process where the quest is for the Other and, in the case of Brazil, the Other is the Indian – literally and symbolically.

There is reference to Lévi-Strauss's work with Amerindian myths – who was himself so profoundly influenced by Jung's ideas – and a plea to restore the repressed and denied Indian part of the Brazilian psyche to consciousness. In this way, the ancestral soul/anima may be revived and from the rich genetic pool or *prima materia* that makes up Brazil's population the alchemical quintessence may be extracted.

Japan

The Japanese analytical psychologist, Hayao Kawai, has written a great deal about his own struggle over many years to transcend the opposites of Japan, on the one hand, and Western culture, many aspects of which he has assimilated, on the other. For this reason, he is uniquely placed to address the subject that he wrote about for *Post-Jungians Today*, in his paper called 'Splitting: resolved or reserved?'

Kawai extrapolates the growing phenomenon of splitting and multiple personality disorder (MPD) from this kind of cultural identity problem which is greatly on the increase in the postmodern age. He warns against treating MPD by trying to integrate the different personalities as this can lead to renewed splitting on the part of the patient. As a result, he is against constellating the *hero archetype* in order to subjugate all of the other parts of the personality and he looks to fairytales to provide material for alternatives to the modern concept of the ego.

The psychological mechanism of splitting leads to experiencing life as a half person and Kawai describes the motif of half persons in fairystories from Japan and Italy. In doing so, he explicates the idea of an individual being led into temptation through the voice of prohibition by a supraordinate power. He concludes that the world is full of half people, that is, people living with a split consciousness, and goes on to say that splitting not only brings about crises but can also help in negotiating them.

Kawai warns that if the therapist seeks to *resolve* the split in the therapeutic encounter, he may set up a split between himself and the patient with the two becoming polarized as the good therapist/bad patient. Kawai suggests instead that it is more helpful for the therapist to *reserve* or act as a container of the split. This can eventually lead to its transformation in the process of self-realization.

Man and His Symbols

The aim of this book has been to communicate some of Jung's complex ideas and the broad scope of his interest in and contribution to a wide variety of areas. These latter include psychology, religion, psychiatry, anthropology, physics, philosophy and sociocultural issues. Throughout the twentieth century, Jung's ideas have seeped into every sphere and many of his terms are in everyday usage. In my experience, there is a growing interest in Jung and I am increasingly asked to recommend reading-matter that makes his ideas more accessible – sometimes by people who do not know that I am an analytical psychologist.

This July I heard the psychoanalyst, Michael Eigon, speak in Dublin and, over the course of an hour, he poured forth a brilliant alchemical medley that incorporated Meister Eckhart, Matte-Blanco (the Infinite is here to stay) and Kerouac, amongst others. When I talked with him after and mentioned that I was a Jungian analyst, his face broke into a delighted grin as he took my hands in his and said: 'I love Jung!'

It feels right to wind down with a short account of how Jung's last book *Man and His Symbols*, came into being. This has a long introduction by Jung in which he puts forward some of his life-long ideas on dreams, symbols, archetypes, typology and the soul. Other chapters include contributions by Joseph Henderson, Marie-Louise von Franz and Aniela Jaffé.

In 1959 Jung agreed to be interviewed by John Freeman for the BBC. According to Freeman, the interview was to be done 'in-depth', in the course of which a warm personal relationship developed between himself and Jung. The programme was deemed a success and Jung received a great deal of correspondence which pleased him greatly as much of it was from people with whom he would normally not have had any contact. One viewer was the managing director of Aldus Books, who asked Freeman if he would suggest to Jung that the latter put down some of his most important ideas in a way that would be accessible to the non-specialist.

Jung met with Freeman and listened carefully to this suggestion, eventually responding with a polite but firm 'No'. However, this was not to be the end of the matter. As we have seen, dreams have always figured prominently in Jung's life, particularly at significant moments. The meeting with Freeman was followed by a dream where Jung found himself 'standing in a public place addressing a great multitude of people who were listening to him with rapt attention and *understanding what he said*' (Jung, 1968: vii).

As a result, he allowed himself to be persuaded to write the book. According to Freeman, Jung devoted the last year of his life almost entirely to it and completed his part of it only 10 days before his final illness and death in 1961. Freeman expresses it as follows:

> At the very end of his own life, which was as full, rich, and happy as any I have ever encountered, he decided to use the strength that was left to him to address his message to a wider public than he had ever tried to reach before. He completed his task and his life in the same month. This book is his legacy to the broad reading public. (Jung, 1968: xii)

The BBC interview itself contained a quote from Jung that has reverberated through the Jungian community ever since. Perhaps what has been written in the foregoing pages will help to illuminate for the reader what Jung may have meant when, in answer to Freeman's question of whether he believed in God, he replied:

> Now? Difficult to answer. I *know*. I don't need to believe. I know.

A Select Bibliography of Jung's Major Writing

The following is a selection of some of Jung's key essays and books which are deliberately not grouped under any specific headings. This is in keeping with Jung's own approach to writing which was to do with expressing ideas rather than propounding theory or technique. These are followed by a few books on Jung by other authors. Both sections number 25 titles in all.

To start with, I have selected papers from the 20 volumes of Jung's *Collected Works* published by Routledge & Kegan Paul, Limited (London). The first few papers will appeal to those readers who are interested in parapsychology and in psychiatry at the Burghölzli at the beginning of the 20th-century with its incorporation of psychoanalysis early on in its inception.

Jung, C.G. (1902) *On the Psychology and Pathology of So-Called Occult Phenomena*. Volume 1.

Jung, C.G. and Riklin F. (1904) *The Associations of Normal Subjects*. Volume 2.

Jung, C.G. (1906) *Psychoanalysis and Association Experiments*. Volume 2.

Jung, C.G. (1914) *The Content of the Psychoses* and *On Psychological Understanding*. Volume 3.

Jung, C.G. (1912) *The Theory of Psychoanalysis*. Volume 4.

The next group of papers show the development of Jung's own ideas that ran concurrent with and followed on from the break with Freud.

Jung, C.G. (1912 and 1956) *Two Kinds of Thinking*; *Symbols of the Mother and of Rebirth*; *The Battle for Deliverance from the Mother*; *The Dual Mother*; *The Sacrifice*. Volume 5.

Jung, C.G. (1921) *General Description of the Types*. Volume 6.

Jung, C.G. (1928) *The Relations between the Ego and the Unconscious*. Volume 7.

The next few papers show the maturing and consolidating of Jung's ideas.

Jung, C.G. (1928) *On Psychic Energy*. Volume 8.

Jung, C.G. (1934) *A Review of the Complex Theory*. Volume 8.

Jung, C.G. (1927/31) *The Structure of the Psyche*. Volume 8.

Jung, C.G. (1947/54) *On the Nature of the Psyche*. Volume 8.

Jung, C.G. (1934/54) *Archetypes of the Collective Unconscious*. Volume 9, Part 1.

Jung, C.G. (1936) *The Concept of the Collective Unconscious*. Volume 9, Part 1.

Jung, C.G. (1938/54) *Psychological Aspects of the Mother Archetype*. Volume 9, Part 1.

Jung, C.G. (1951) *The Ego, The Shadow, The Syzygy: Anima and Animus, The Self, Christ, a Symbol of the Self*. Volume 9, Part II.

Jung, C.G. (1952) *Answer to Job*. Volume 11.

The following two papers are on psychology and alchemy.

Jung, C.G. (1929) *Commentary on 'The Secret of the Golden Flower'*. Volume 12.

Jung, C.G. (1946) *The Psychology of the Transference*. Volume 16.

These books by Jung are not part of the *Collected Works*.

Jung, C.G. (ed.) (1964) *Man and His Symbols*. New York: Dell Publishing.
Jung, C.G. (1968) *Analytical Psychology: Its Theory and Practice*. New York: Random House.
Jung, C.G. (1933) *Modern Man in Search of a Soul*. London: Routledge & Kegan Paul.

The last three books are by other analytical psychologists. The first is a scholarly but accessible work on Jung's psychology centred in mythology, history and western culture. I gave it a glowing review in *The Economist*, when it first appeared.

Zoja, L. (1995) *Growth and Guilt: Psychology and the Limits of Development*. London: Routledge.

The next book is a beautifully written 'in-depth' but highly accessible account of some of Jung's most complex ideas.

Stein, M. (1998) *Jung's Map of the Soul*. Peru, Illinois: Open Court.

The last book is a very readable narrative history of the Jungian community worldwide.

Kirsch, T. (2000) *The Jungians: A Comparative and Historical Perspective*. London: Routledge.

Forthcoming

Hinshaw, R. (2000) *Essays on Jung's Psychology*. Einsielden, Switzerland: Daimon.
Shamdasani, S. *Prisms of Psychology: Jung and History*. Work in progress.

References

Adler, G. (ed.) (1976) *C.G. Jung Letters*. London: Routledge & Kegan Paul.

Adler, G. (1978) *Reflections on 'Chance', 'Fate', and 'Synchronicity'*. Unpublished.

Astor, J. (1995) *Michael Fordham: Innovations in Analytical Psychology*. London: Routledge.

Beebe, J. (1992) 'Jung on the Masculine: An Introduction', in R. Papadopoulos (ed.), *Carl Gustav Jung: Critical Assessments*. London: Routledge. pp. 367–75.

Bennet, E.A. (1961) *C.G. Jung*. London: Barrie Books.

Cambray, J. (2000) *Enactments and Amplification*. In press with the *Journal of Analytical Psychology*.

Carotenuto, A. (1982) *A Secret Symmetry: Sabina Speilrein*. New York: Dell Publishing.

Casement, A. (1995) 'A Brief History of Jungian Splits in the U.K.', *Journal of Analytical Psychology*, 40: 327–42.

Casement, A. (ed.) (1998) *Post-Jungians Today: Key Papers in Contemporary Analytical Psychology*. London: Routledge.

Clarke, J.J. (1992) *In Search of Jung: Historical and Philosophical Enquiries*. London: Routledge.

Cocks, G. (1997) *Psychothcrapy in the Third Reich: The Göring Institute*. New Brunswick, New Jersey: Transaction Publishers.

Edinger, E.F. (1986) *Encounter with the Self*. Toronto: Inner City Books.

Ellenberger, H.F. (1970) *The Discovery of the Unconscious: The History and Evolution of Dynamic Psychiatry*. New York: Basic Books.

Fordham, M. (1993) *The Making of an Analyst: A Memoir*. London: Free Association Books.

Freud, S. (1966) *On the History of the Psycho-Analytic Movement*. London and New York: W.W. Norton & Co.

Friedman, M.S. (1986) *Martin Buber and the Eternal*. New York: Human Sciences Press.

Friedman, M.S. (1991) *Martin Buber's Encounter on the Narrow Ridge: A Life*. New York: Paragon House.

Gottlieb, F. (1994) 'The Kabbala, Jung and the feminine', in J. Ryce-Menuhin (ed.), *Jung and the Monotheisms: Judaism, Christianity and Islam*. London: Routledge.

Guggenbühl-Craig, A. (1977) *Marriage – Dead or Alive*. Zurich: Spring.

Hanegraaf, W.J. (1998) *New Age Religion and Western Culture: Esotericism in the Mirror of Secular Thought*. Albany, NY: SUNY Press.

Hauke, C. (2000) *Jung and the Postmodern: The Interpretation of Realities*. London: Routledge.

Humbert, E.G. (1984) *C.G. Jung: The Fundamentals of Theory and Practice*. Wilmette, Illinois: Chiron Publications.

Jaffé A. (1989) *From the Life and Works of C.G. Jung*. Einsiedeln, Switzerland: Daimon.

Jarrett, J. (ed.) (1988) *Nietzsche's Zazrathustra: Notes of the Seminar Given in 1934–1939 by C.G. Jung*. Princeton, NJ: Princeton University Press.

Jarrett, J. (1992) 'Dialectic as "Tao" in Plato and Jung', in P. Papadopoulos (ed.), *Carl Gustav Jung: Critical Assessments*. London: Routledge. pp. 11–26.

Jones, E. (1953) *Sigmund Freud: Life and Work*. Volume I. London: The Hogarth Press.

Jones, E. (1955) *Sigmund Freud: Life and Work*. Volume II. London: The Hogarth Press.
Jones, E. (1957) *Sigmund Freud: Life and Work*. Volume III. London: The Hogarth Press.
Jones, E. (1959) *Free Associations*. London: The Hogarth Press.

Jung's Collected Works

Jung, C.G. (1957) *Psychiatric Studies*. Volume 1. London: Routledge & Kegan Paul.
Jung, C.G. (1973) *Experimental Researches*. Volume 2. London: Routledge & Kegan Paul.
Jung, C.G. (1960a) *The Psychogenesis of Mental Disease*. Volume 3. London: Routledge & Kegan Paul.
Jung, C.G. (1961) *Freud and Psychoanalysis*. Volume 4. London: Routledge & Kegan Paul.
Jung, C.G. (1971) *Psychological Types*. Volume 6. London: Routledge & Kegan Paul.
Jung, C.G. (1960b) *The Structure and Dynamics of the Psyche*. Volume 8. London: Routledge & Kegan Paul.
Jung, C.G. (1959a) *The Archetypes and the Collective Unconscious*. Volume 9. Part I. London: Routledge & Kegan Paul.
Jung, C.G. (1953a) *Psychology and Alchemy*. Volume 12. London: Routledge & Kegan Paul.
Jung, C.G. (1967) *Alchemical Studies*. Volume 13. London: Routledge & Kegan Paul.
Jung, C.G. (1963a) *Mysterium Coniunctionis*. Volume 14. London: Routledge & Kegan Paul.
Jung, C.G. (1954) *The Practice of Psychotherapy*. Volume 16. London: Routledge & Kegan Paul.
Jung, C.G. (1977) *The Symbolic Life*. Volume 18. London: Routledge & Kegan Paul.

Other Works by Jung

Jung, C.G. (1953b) *Two Essays on Analytical Psychology*. New York. Bollingen Foundation Inc.
Jung, C.G. (1956) *Symbols of Transformation*. Princeton, New Jersey: Princeton University Press.
Jung, C.G. (1958) *Answer to Job*. Princeton, New Jersey: Princeton University Press.
Jung, C.G. (1959b) *Aion: Researches into the Phenomenology of the Self*. Princeton, New Jersey: Princeton University Press.
Jung, C.G. (1963b) *Memories, Dreams, Reflections*. London: Routledge & Kegan Paul.
Jung, C.G. (1966) *Two Essays on Analytical Psychology*. Princeton, New Jersey: Princeton University Press.
Jung, C.G. (ed.) (1968) *Man and His Symbols*. New York: Dell Publishing.
Jung, C.G. (1991) *Psychology of the Unconscious: A Study of the Transformations and Symbolisms of the Libido*. London: Routledge.
Kerr, J. (1994) *A Most Dangerous Method: The Story of Jung, Freud and Sabina Spielrein*. London: Sinclair-Stevenson.
King, P. and Steiner R. (eds) (1991) *The Freud–Klein Controversies 1941–45*. London: Routledge.
Kirsch, J. (1982) 'Carl Gustav Jung and the Jews: The Real Story', *Journal of Psychology and Judaism*, 6 (2): 113–43.
Kirsch, T. (2000) *The Jungians: A Comparative and Historical Perspective*. London: Routledge.
Lothane, Z. (1999) 'Tender Love and Transference: Unpublished Letters of C.G. Jung and Sabina Spielrein', *International Journal of Psychoanalysis*, 80: 1189–1204.
Maguire, W. (ed.) (1974) *The Freud/Jung Letters*. London: The Hogarth Press.
Maidenbaum, A. and Martin A. (1991) *Lingering Shadows: Jungians, Freudians, and Anti-Semitism*. Boston: Shambala Publications.

Nagy, M. (1991) *Philosophical Issues in the Psychology of C.G. Jung*. Albany: State University of New York Press.

Papadopoulos, R. (1992) *Carl Gustav Jung: Critical Assessments*. London: Routledge.

Ryce-Menuhin, J. (1994) *Jung and the Monotheisms: Judaism, Christianity and Islam*. London: Routledge.

Samuels, A. (1993) *The Political Psyche*. London: Routledge.

Samuels, A., Shorter, B., Plaut, A. (1986) *A Critical Dictionary of Jungian Analysis*. London: Routledge & Kegan Paul.

Schaeder, G. (1973) *The Hebrew Humanism of Martin Buber*. Detroit: Wayne State University.

Schlamm, L. *James Hillman's School of Archetypal Psychology and Polytheistic Theology, Psychology and Religion*. Unpublished.

Schopenhauer, A. (1883) *The World as Will and Idea*. Volume III. Translated by R.B. Haldane and J. Kemp. London: Routledge & Kegan Paul.

Schwartz-Salant, N. (1989) *The Borderline Personality: Vision and Healing*. Wilmette, Illinois: Chiron Publications.

Segal, R. (1992) *The Gnostic Jung*. London: Routledge.

Shamdasani, S. (1990) 'A Woman Called Frank', *A Journal of Archetype and Culture*, 50: 26–56.

Shamdasani, S. (1993) 'Automatic Writing and the Discovery of the Unconscious', *A Journal of Archetype and Culture*, 54: 100–31.

Shamdasani, S. (1995) 'Memories, Dreams, Omissions', *A Journal of Archetype and Culture*, 57: 115–37.

Shamdasani, S. (1998a) 'From Geneva to Zurich: Jung and French Switzerland', *The Journal of Analytical Psychology*, 43: 115–26.

Shamdasani, S. (1998b) *Cult Fictions: C.G. Jung and the Founding of Analytical Psychology*. London: Routledge.

Singer Harris, A. (1996) *Living with Paradox: An Introduction to Jungian Psychology*. Stanford, CA: Wadsworth.

Stein, M. (1985) *Jung's Treatment of Christianity: The Psychotherapy of a Religious Tradition*. Wilmette, Illinois: Chiron Publications.

Stein, M. (1998) *Jung's Map of the Soul*. Peru, Illinois: Open Court Publishing.

Stepansky, P.E. (1992) 'The Empiricist as Rebel: Jung, Freud and the Burdens of Discipleship', in R. Papadopoulos (ed.), *Carl Gustav Jung: Critical Assessments*. London: Routledge. pp. 169–99.

Tacey, D. (1998) 'Twisting and turning with James Hillman', in A. Casement (ed.), *Post-Jungians Today*. London: Routledge. pp. 215–34.

Taylor, E. (1998) 'Jung before Freud, not Freud before Jung', *Journal of Analytical Psychology*, 43 (1): 97–114.

Taylor, E. (1999) *Shadow Culture: Psychology and Spirituality in America*. Washington, DC: Counterpoint.

White, V. (1961) *God and the Unconscious*. London: Meridian Books.

Winnicott, D. (1964) 'Review of *Memories, Dreams Reflections*', *The Journal of Psychoanalysis*, 45: 450–5.

Wittels, F. (1934) *Sigmund Freud*. London: Allen & Unwin.

Zabriskie, B.D. (1992) 'The Feminine: Pre and Post-Jungian', in R. Papadopoulos (ed.), *Carl Gustav Jung: Critical Assessments*. London: Routledge. pp. 376–90.

Index